THE ART OF SETTING BOUNDARIES

A Step-by-Step Guide to Manage Stress, Focus on What Truly Matters, and Say No With Confidence

Alex Harper

Book Cover by Alex Harper

Illustrations by Alex Harper

First edition 2024

CONTENTS

MAKE A DIFFERENCE WITH YOUR REVIEW

Your Words Can Change Someone's Life

"If someone gets upset because you set a boundary, it's even more proof you needed it." – Unknown

We all want to live happier, healthier lives, but it's not always easy. Sometimes, we struggle to say "no" because we worry about disappointing others. That's why I wrote *The Art of Setting Boundaries*. It's a simple, step-by-step guide to help anyone—yes, even you—start protecting your time, energy, and peace.

But there are so many people still searching for help. That's where you come in.

Would you lend a hand to someone just like you—someone overwhelmed, stressed, or ready to take charge of their life?

Your review could be the push they need to start their own boundary-setting journey.

Most people choose books based on reviews.

Leaving a review costs nothing. It takes less than a minute, but it can make a big difference. Your words could help:

- A parent find time for themselves again.

- A young adult finally say "no" without feeling guilty.

- A professional balance their endless to-do list.

- An empath create space to breathe.

- Someone heal and rebuild their life.

Ready to help?

1. Simply scan the QR code below or visit this link:
   The Art of Setting Boundaries

2. Leave a quick review sharing what you learned or how the book helped you.

Your voice matters. Your kindness matters.

Thank you for being someone who helps others find peace, confidence, and clarity. It means the world to me.

With gratitude,

Alex Harper

INTRODUCTION

Years ago, I found myself standing on the edge of a conversation I didn't want to have. My friend, bless her heart, was asking for yet another favor that I simply didn't have the capacity to give; as I nodded my head and agreed, a familiar knot formed in my stomach. That knot was made of resentment, fatigue, and the faint whisper of self-betrayal. I went home that night and sat on the couch, wondering why saying "no" felt like a Herculean task.

That moment was my wake-up call. It was the beginning of my journey towards understanding the importance of boundaries. I realized that boundaries aren't walls meant to keep others out but paths that allow us to navigate relationships with kindness and respect—for ourselves and others.

Many of us struggle with saying "no." We think we're selfish or mean, but we're just human. According to recent studies, an overwhelming number of people report feeling stressed and overwhelmed due to their inability to set boundaries. This is a widespread issue that affects our mental health, relationships, and overall well-being. We are conditioned to be agreeable, not rock the boat, and to keep everyone else happy. But this often comes at the expense of our own peace and happiness.

This book is for you. Whether you are a young adult trying to find your voice, a professional juggling endless demands, a parent needing to carve out time for yourself, or an empath feeling overwhelmed by others' emotions—boundaries are crucial. They are essential for individuals healing from trauma or codependency, as they help create a safe space to grow and heal.

The purpose of this book is to change the narrative around boundary-setting. It's not about being selfish; it's about empowerment and self-care. I want to guide you through practical tools and culturally sensitive strategies that you can use in your life. There will be interactive exercises to help you integrate these tools so you can start saying "no" with confidence and focus on what truly matters to you.

What sets this book apart? Well, I've packed it with psychological insights and expert advice. You'll find real-life examples and relatable case studies that illustrate key concepts. These elements are designed to help you see the transformative power of boundaries and how they can enhance your relationships and personal autonomy.

Throughout the book, you'll learn how to build self-confidence, manage stress, and improve your communication skills. We'll start by understanding what boundaries are and why they're essential. Then, we'll move on to practical steps for setting and maintaining them. It's a journey from awareness to application, and it's one that promises personal growth.

My vision for writing this book is simple: I want to help you achieve healthier relationships and personal growth. I'm passionate about offering guidance that anyone can follow. I believe in the power of boundaries to lead to greater self-respect and emotional resilience. This isn't just a book; it's a path to a more fulfilling life where you can thrive instead of just survive.

I invite you to join me on this journey. Open your mind and embrace the transformative power of setting boundaries. Let's work together to make saying "no" a tool for empowerment and lasting change. You deserve to live a life that reflects your values and needs, and this book is here to help you do just that.

UNDERSTANDING BOUNDARIES

HAVE YOU EVER FOUND yourself tangled in a web of obligations and wondered how you ended up there? There I was, knee-deep in my own mess, attending yet another committee meeting I had no interest in, wondering if there was a polite way to fake my own demise to escape. I mean, how did I become the go-to person for organizing the annual neighborhood bake sale when I can't even bake? Somewhere along the way, I forgot that "no" was an option, and my boundaries were as nonexistent as my cake-baking skills. This got me thinking: why do we find it so hard to say no? Many of us are caught in a never-ending cycle of yeses, afraid that a "no" might make us seem selfish or unreliable. But what if I told you that boundaries are actually your best friend, not the enemy?

Setting boundaries is crucial for maintaining sanity, especially in a world that seems intent on stretching us thin. The concept of boundaries is like an invisible security guard standing at the entrance of your personal space, politely but firmly saying, "Sorry, you're not on the list," to the unwanted stressors of life. Boundaries are the unsung heroes of emotional and mental well-being, silently protecting your personal limits in everything from emotions to physical space. Understanding and defining these boundaries is the first step to reclaiming your time, energy, and peace of mind.

Defining Boundaries: The Basics

Boundaries are those elusive, invisible lines that define what is acceptable for you in various aspects of life—be it emotional, physical, or mental. Think of them as the rules of engagement in the game of life, where you get to decide what players can or cannot do within your personal space. Emotional boundaries, for instance, help maintain your sanity by deciding what feelings and personal information you're willing to share with others. They act as a protective shield for your emotional well-being, ensuring that others' expectations or demands don't trample your feelings. On the other hand, physical boundaries involve your personal space and comfort with physical interactions, which can vary greatly from person to person. They help you assert your right to personal space and bodily autonomy, much like a "no trespassing" sign for your physical being.

In the same way, we differentiate between emotional and physical boundaries, it's essential to understand what healthy versus unhealthy boundaries look like. Healthy boundaries are flexible yet firm, adapting to different situations without losing their core purpose of protecting your well-being. They allow you to engage in relationships and activities without feeling overwhelmed or compromised. Unhealthy boundaries, however, are either too rigid or too porous, leading to feelings of isolation or being taken advantage of. For example, consistently putting others' needs above your own to the point of exhaustion is a sign of unhealthy boundaries. On the flip side, refusing to engage with others out of fear of being hurt can be equally damaging. Striking a balance is key to maintaining healthy boundaries that serve you well.

Boundaries play a pivotal role in our daily lives, influencing everything from personal well-being to stress management. By setting clear boundaries, you take charge of your life, deciding what you will and will not accept. This act of self-care is not selfish; it's a necessary step in managing stress and maintaining your sanity in a world that often demands too much. Boundaries help prioritize your needs, ensuring you're not constantly running on empty. They serve as a buffer zone, allowing you to recharge and focus on what truly matters.

Moreover, boundaries are a declaration of autonomy and empowerment. They are a testament to your self-respect, allowing you to assert your needs and make decisions that align with your values. When you establish boundaries, you take control of your life, enhancing your ability to make decisions without being swayed by external pressures. This empowerment leads to greater self-confidence and a clearer sense of identity, helping you navigate life's challenges with ease.

Boundaries also reflect your personal identity and values, acting as a mirror of who you are and what you stand for. They align with your core beliefs, allowing you to live authentically and stay true to yourself. By setting boundaries that resonate with your values, you create a life that reflects your true self, not a life dictated by others' expectations. This alignment brings a sense of fulfillment and contentment as you live following your principles and priorities. So, as you embark on this exploration of boundaries, remember that they are not just lines in the sand; they are the foundation of a well-lived life where you are the author of your own story.

The Psychology Behind Boundary Issues

I must confess, my relationship with boundaries has been a bit like trying to train a particularly willful dog—lots of trial and error, with a few successful moments. Why, you ask? Because the roots of boundary issues often run deep and are tangled with our past experiences and personality quirks. It's like that old sweater you can't quite part with because it's knitted with memories, good and bad. Our early experiences, particularly childhood, play a significant role in shaping how we approach boundaries. If you grew up in an environment where personal limits were not respected, setting boundaries as an adult can feel as mysterious and intimidating as deciphering ancient runes.

Childhood experiences are like the blueprint for our boundary-setting behaviors. Suppose you were lucky enough to grow up in a supportive environment. In that case, you might find boundary-setting to be second nature. However, for many, childhood may have involved blurred lines where personal space and autonomy were not recognized. This often leads to patterns where boundaries either don't exist or they are so rigid that they block out meaningful connections. It's not uncommon to see adults who, as children, learned that their needs were secondary struggle to assert themselves and establish healthy limits.

Now, let's talk about the psychological roadblocks that often pop up like annoying speed bumps on our path to boundary-setting. Fear of rejection is a big one. It's human nature to want to be liked, and the idea of someone disapproving because you said "no" can feel like being sent to the social equivalent of Siberia. This fear can paralyze us, making boundary-setting feel like a dangerous game. Then there's guilt. Ah, guilt—that pesky emotion convincing you that asserting your needs is wrong or selfish. It whispers in your ear, urging you to prioritize others, even if it leaves you burnt out and resentful.

Mental health conditions can further complicate this already tricky landscape. Anxiety, for instance, is like a relentless critic that questions every decision, making boundary-setting feel like walking a tightrope over a pit of alligators. Those with anxiety might avoid setting boundaries to prevent potential conflict, even if it means sacrificing their own peace. On the flip side, depression often leads to boundary permeability, where the line between self and others becomes so blurred that one's own needs get lost in translation. The feeling of worthlessness associated with depression can make it hard to believe that your boundaries are valid or deserve to be respected.

But here's the silver lining: understanding these psychological influences gives us the power to address and overcome them. Cognitive-behavioral approaches, for example, offer a practical toolkit for reinforcing boundaries. By challenging negative thoughts and replacing them with empowering beliefs, you can redefine your approach to boundary-setting. Think of it as upgrading your mental software to version 2.0—a version where you can handle life's demands with clarity and confidence.

Imagine a scenario where you consistently say "yes" to your boss's last-minute requests, even when it means sacrificing your personal time. It's easy to see how this can lead to resentment and burnout. By applying cognitive-behavioral techniques, you can start by identifying the thought patterns that lead you to overcommit, such as the fear of disappointing your boss. Then, you work on reframing those thoughts, recognizing that setting limits is not a sign of incompetence but a necessary step for maintaining your well-being and productivity. Over time, these new, healthier patterns become second nature, and you find yourself more capable of setting boundaries without the burden of guilt or anxiety.

Understanding the psychology behind boundary issues is like having a map to navigate the often confusing terrain of human interactions. It enables you to recognize the factors that hold you back and equips you with the tools to move forward. So, as you reflect on your own boundary-setting challenges, remember that change is possible. With a bit of patience and practice, you can transform how you engage with the world.

Cultural Influences on Boundary-Setting

Picture this: you're at a family gathering, and your aunt insists you have another serving of her famous casserole. You politely decline, but she's not taking no for an answer. In some cultures, turning down food might be seen as offensive, while in others, refusing without a second thought is perfectly fine. This little scenario only scratches the surface of how cultural backgrounds influence how we perceive and set boundaries. When we talk about boundaries, it's important to remember that the rules aren't the same everywhere. This can be confusing when different cultural expectations collide.

In individualistic cultures like those in the West, personal autonomy and clear communication are often celebrated. Here, boundaries are more explicit, with a strong emphasis on personal space and individual rights. People are generally encouraged to speak up for themselves and assert their needs directly. This cultural norm supports boundary-setting in a straightforward manner, where saying "no" is not only accepted but sometimes expected. The focus is on individual rights, and maintaining personal boundaries is seen as a sign of self-respect.

Contrast this with collectivist cultures, where the focus is on community and collective well-being. Here, boundaries might be more subtle, with a greater emphasis on harmony and conformity. In these settings, saying "no" could be perceived as disruptive or disrespectful, which means people often set boundaries in more indirect ways. The family unit holds great significance, and extended family members are frequently involved in personal decisions. This can create a delicate dance of maintaining personal boundaries while respecting familial ties and obligations.

Societal norms, too, play a significant role in shaping how we set boundaries. Gender roles are a prime example. In many societies, traditional gender expectations can dictate how boundaries are perceived and communicated. Women, for instance, might be socialized to be more nurturing and accommodating, which can make it challenging to assert boundaries without feeling guilty or selfish. On the other hand, men might face societal pressure to be tough and self-sufficient, potentially making it harder for them to express vulnerability or ask for help when needed. These gendered expectations can create unique challenges in boundary-setting as individuals strive to balance societal norms with their personal needs.

Similarly, societal expectations around family obligations can significantly impact boundary-setting behaviors. In many cultures, family expectations can be demanding, with individuals feeling obligated to prioritize family needs over their own. This can lead to blurred boundaries, where personal desires are often set aside to maintain familial harmony. The pressure to conform to these expectations can be intense, making it difficult for individuals to assert their boundaries without feeling like they are letting their family down.

Navigating cross-cultural boundaries adds another layer of complexity to the mix. When people from different cultural backgrounds interact, misunderstandings often occur due to differing expectations and norms. What might be considered a polite boundary in one culture could be seen as rude or aggressive in another. This cultural clash can lead to tension and conflict, making it crucial to approach cross-cultural interactions with sensitivity and an open mind. Understanding and respecting cultural differences in boundary-setting can enhance interpersonal effectiveness and create a more respectful environment.

To effectively set boundaries in multicultural environments, it's helpful to be adaptable and culturally sensitive. One strategy is cultivating self-awareness and reflecting on how your cultural background influences your boundary-setting behaviors. This self-awareness can help you identify potential areas of conflict and guide you in adapting your approach. Additionally, tailoring boundary-setting techniques to align with cultural norms can facilitate smoother interactions. For example, in more hierarchical cultures, using formal language and respecting authority can help navigate professional boundaries effectively.

Ultimately, setting boundaries in a culturally diverse world requires a delicate balance of asserting personal needs while respecting cultural norms. By embracing cultural differences and adapting communication strategies accordingly, you can navigate the complexities of cross-cultural boundary-setting with greater ease and understanding.

Boundary-Setting Myths and Misconceptions

Imagine this: you've finally mustered the courage to say no to your neighbor's request to babysit their overly energetic dog—who once mistook your couch for a chew toy—only to be met with a look of disbelief and perhaps a whisper of "selfish" behind your back. Sound familiar? It's a scenario many of us dread, yet it's built on a myth as old as time itself. There's this pervasive idea that setting boundaries is inherently selfish as if looking after your own needs means you're suddenly the villain in everyone else's story. But here's the truth: boundaries are not about shutting others out; they're about letting yourself in. They are about carving out a space where your needs, emotions, and time are respected, not trampled on.

Another popular myth suggests that boundaries are relationship kryptonite, the very thing that will poison your connections and leave you isolated. Talk about dramatic! The reality is quite the opposite. Healthy boundaries are like the invisible threads that keep relationships strong and vibrant. They help prevent the kind of resentment that festers when one party feels overburdened or unappreciated. Without boundaries, relationships can quickly become one-sided affairs where one person's needs overshadow the other's. When both parties know where they stand, it creates a foundation of trust and respect. Letting go of this myth opens the door to mutually fulfilling and nurturing relationships.

Misunderstandings around boundary-setting don't just strain relationships; they can also wreak havoc on your mental well-being. When boundaries are absent, stress levels can skyrocket. You're left playing an endless game of emotional dodgeball, trying to avoid the ball while juggling everyone else's expectations. It's exhausting and entirely unsustainable. Facing constant pressure to meet others' needs without regard for your own can lead to burnout and a loss of self. In this state, you're not just helping others; you're sacrificing your own happiness and peace of mind.

Now, let's clear the air between healthy boundaries and rigid barriers. Healthy boundaries are like a well-tuned instrument, adapting to the situation at hand while maintaining their core function. They allow you to engage with the world flexibly, confident in your ability to protect your needs. Rigid barriers, however, are more like a fortress, impenetrable and isolating, cutting you off from meaningful connections as much as they protect you. Learning to distinguish between the two can transform how you interact with others, allowing you to maintain your integrity while being open to change.

Research has shown that setting boundaries is beneficial and necessary for personal health and relationship satisfaction. For instance, studies indicate that clear boundaries contribute to lower stress levels and increased well-being. This is because boundaries help manage emotional overload, protecting you from the burnout that comes from overextending yourself. By setting limits, you not only protect yourself but also set an example for others, encouraging them to do the same.

So, how do we shift this narrative and embrace boundary-setting as a positive force? It starts with redefining the conversation around boundaries. Visualize them as empowering tools that enhance your life and relationships rather than detract from them. Consider the story of a friend who learned to set boundaries at work, saying no to extra projects that interfered with personal time. Not only did she find herself with more energy and enthusiasm for her job, but her relationship with her boss improved as clear expectations were set. This is the power of boundaries—they pave the way for clarity, understanding, and respect.

In conclusion, boundaries are not the enemy; they are allies in the journey to a fulfilling life. They are the keys to unlocking healthier relationships, reducing stress, and fostering personal growth. Embrace them as an integral part of self-care, and watch as your interactions transform. As you move forward, remember that boundaries are not just lines you draw; they are expressions of your values, needs, and self-worth. With each boundary you set, you take a step toward living a life that genuinely reflects who you are.

Emotional Resilience and Self-Care

Some days, life feels like an episode of a soap opera I didn't sign up for. One minute, you're sipping your morning coffee; the next, you're in the midst of an emotional whirlwind involving a forgotten deadline, a toddler tantrum, and your neighbor's cat who insists on treating your garden like a public restroom. It's in moments like these that emotional resilience becomes your best ally. Emotional resilience is like that stretchy yoga band you use to (attempt to) limber up—it's your ability to bounce back from life's curveballs without snapping. It's the psychological muscle that helps you recover quickly from difficulties, and believe me, it's the key to maintaining those boundaries we worked so hard to set.

Emotional resilience is crucial in boundary-setting because it fortifies you against the inevitable pushback and challenges. Imagine it as the sturdy scaffolding that supports your boundary wall while you work on reinforcing the brick and mortar. Resilience allows you to stand firm when someone tries to bulldoze your "no," and it helps you bounce back when life throws a wrecking ball your way. For instance, consider a time when you had to enforce a boundary with a friend who constantly borrowed your things without asking. It might have been uncomfortable, but your resilience helped you handle the situation gracefully, turning a potentially awkward confrontation into a teachable moment for both of you.

Several factors contribute to building this kind of resilience, and they're more accessible than you might think. Internally, fostering a positive self-talk habit is like giving your inner cheerleader a megaphone. When you face challenges, self-talk can transform "I can't handle this" into "I've got this." It's about recognizing that your mind is like a radio station, and you have the power to change the channel from "endless negativity" to "positivity central." Externally, supportive relationships act as the safety net that catches you when you stumble. Surrounding yourself with people who believe in you is like having your own personal pit crew ready to refuel and cheer you on every step of the way.

Building emotional resilience also involves practical strategies that you can start implementing today. Let's talk about journaling and reflection. Keep a journal handy—not just for penning your next big novel, but as a tool for reflection. Writing down your thoughts can help you process emotions and spot patterns in your boundary-setting efforts. Then there's the growth mindset, a concept that's all about believing in your ability to improve and adapt. Approach each boundary-setting challenge as an opportunity to learn rather than a potential failure. Remember, every setback is a setup for a comeback.

Let me tell you about Lisa, a young professional overwhelmed by her boss's constant demands. Initially, Lisa struggled with saying no, fearing it would harm her career. However, she learned to assert her boundaries effectively by building her emotional resilience. Lisa started practicing positive self-talk, telling herself that setting limits was not a weakness but a strength. She also sought support from a mentor who encouraged her to communicate her boundaries clearly. Through journaling, Lisa reflected on her progress and adjusted her strategies as needed. Over time, she noticed a significant improvement not only in her stress levels but also in her work relationships. Lisa's story is a testament to the power of resilience in overcoming boundary challenges.

Developing emotional resilience is akin to training for a marathon, except you're running the race of life—and this race has no finish line. You'll face hurdles, unexpected detours, and maybe a few metaphorical rainstorms. Still, each step forward strengthens your ability to handle whatever comes your way. By cultivating resilience, you equip yourself with the tools to maintain your boundaries even when the going gets tough. So, grab your metaphorical running shoes, embrace the process, and remember: you're stronger than you think and more resilient than you ever imagined.

Reflection Exercise: Building Your Resilience Toolkit

Take a moment to reflect on a recent situation where you faced a boundary challenge. What internal dialogue did you have? How did supportive relationships play a role? Jot down your thoughts and identify one positive self-talk statement and one supportive relationship you can lean on moving forward. This exercise is your starting point for building a personalized resilience toolkit to support your boundary-setting journey.

Self-Care as a Boundary Foundation

Consider this scenario: you're in an airplane, and the flight attendant demonstrates safety procedures. Remember how they always instruct you to put on your own oxygen mask before helping others? Self-care is your life's oxygen mask. It's not just bubble baths and spa days—though those are delightful—it's about implementing daily practices that ensure your well-being so you have the energy and capacity to face life's challenges. Self-care is the cornerstone of effective boundary-setting because it requires you to recognize and prioritize your needs, much like deciding to wear pants before leaving the house.

Self-care comes in various flavors, each as vital as the next: physical, emotional, and spiritual. Physical self-care is about nourishing your body, whether taking a brisk walk to clear your mind or eating a balanced diet that doesn't solely consist of coffee and leftover pizza (guilty as charged). Emotional self-care involves acknowledging and processing your feelings, allowing yourself to experience the full spectrum of human emotion without judgment. It's giving yourself permission to cry during a sappy movie because, let's face it, sometimes a good cry is as cathartic as a comedy marathon. Spiritual self-care doesn't necessarily mean meditating on a mountaintop, though that sounds lovely. It can be any practice that connects you to something larger than yourself, like reading, prayer, or simply appreciating the beauty of nature.

Integrating self-care into your routine is like adding a sturdy fence around your personal space, reinforcing your boundaries, and preventing burnout. Establishing daily routines that prioritize your needs—like turning off work emails after 7 PM or setting aside a few minutes each morning for quiet reflection—are proactive boundary measures. These routines act as gentle reminders that your well-being is non-negotiable. When you regularly engage in self-care, you're telling yourself and the world that you matter, that your time and energy are valuable, and that you refuse to be the world's doormat.

Practical self-care strategies are as varied as your favorite ice cream flavors. Scheduling downtime is one approach—consider it a mini-vacation for your mind and spirit. Whether it's a weekend getaway or simply an afternoon spent exploring a new hobby, this downtime is crucial. Personal retreats don't need to be elaborate; sometimes, they can be as simple as a quiet afternoon with a good book or a leisurely stroll through the park. These moments recharge your energy levels, allowing you to tackle whatever life throws your way with renewed vigor.

Yet, despite its importance, self-care often gets a bad rap as being indulgent or selfish. There's a common misconception that taking time for yourself is akin to shirking responsibilities. But let's challenge that notion right now. Self-care is not about escapism; it's about sustainability. It's about ensuring that you have the resources to meet the demands of life without depleting your reserves. Consider it maintenance for your soul, much like you might take your car in for a regular tune-up. Just as ignoring a car's maintenance needs can lead to a breakdown, neglecting self-care can leave you running on fumes and unable to set or uphold boundaries effectively.

So, next time you're tempted to skip that yoga class or forgo your evening walk, remember that self-care is not a luxury but a necessity. It's the bedrock upon which your boundaries stand firm. Embracing self-care is a step toward living authentically, ensuring your needs are met so you can show up fully in all areas of your life.

Mindfulness Techniques for Boundary Awareness

There I was, sitting in traffic, gripping the steering wheel like it owed me money, when it hit me: I was living life on autopilot. I was reacting to everything and everyone, from my morning coffee to my boss's latest request, without pausing to consider my own needs. Enter mindfulness—a practice that taught me to hit the pause button and actually notice my life instead of letting it whiz by. Mindfulness is like having a friendly referee in your brain, reminding you to check in with yourself before committing to yet another weekend of obligatory social events. It's about being present in the moment, fully aware of your surroundings and feelings, and it's a game-changer for boundary awareness. Mindfulness helps you tune into the subtle cues your body and mind send when you're about to overcommit or let someone bulldoze your personal space. It's like upgrading from an old-school flip phone to the latest smartphone—suddenly, you can see everything in vibrant detail.

The beauty of mindfulness is that it's not about sitting cross-legged on a mountaintop (unless that's your thing). It's about finding moments of presence in everyday life. Mindfulness meditation, for example, is a simple yet powerful practice that enhances your awareness of the present moment. By focusing on your breath and observing your thoughts without judgment, you cultivate an acute awareness of your personal limits and needs. It's like defogging the windshield of your mind, allowing you to see where you're going and what obstacles might lie ahead. This heightened awareness makes it easier to detect when a boundary is being crossed or when you're about to say yes when you really mean no.

One of my favorite mindfulness exercises is the body scan meditation. Picture it as a gentle, internal MRI that helps you detect physical tension and stress, which often accompany boundary violations. By slowly focusing on each part of your body, you can identify areas that feel tight or uncomfortable, hinting at stressors you might not be consciously aware of. It's like having a conversation with your body, asking it how it's doing, and actually listening to the response. Breathing exercises also work wonders for calming stress responses. Taking slow, deep breaths signals to your nervous system that it's okay to relax, which is particularly handy when you're faced with a boundary challenge. Imagine taking a few deep breaths before responding to a demanding email; it's incredible how a little oxygen can transform your response from reactive to reflective.

Regular mindfulness practice doesn't just make you more aware of your boundaries; it strengthens them. It's like going to the mental gym, building your emotional muscles so they're ready to hold firm when needed. Mindfulness improves focus and clarity, making decision-making more manageable and more deliberate. It's like having your very own mental GPS guiding you through the maze of life's demands with precision. When your mind is clear, you're better equipped to assess situations and decide whether they align with your values and boundaries. This clarity empowers you to make decisions prioritizing your well-being, reducing the likelihood of overcommitting or feeling overwhelmed.

If you're wondering how to start incorporating mindfulness into your routine, don't worry—it's simpler than you think. Begin by setting up a daily mindfulness practice schedule. Start small, like five minutes a day, and gradually increase the time as you become more comfortable. You can practice mindfulness in the morning to set a positive tone for the day or use it as a mid-day reset when things start to feel chaotic. The key is consistency, much like watering a plant regularly helps it grow. Over time, mindfulness becomes a natural part of your life, enhancing your boundary awareness and resilience like a trusty sidekick always by your side.

Cultivating Inner Peace Through Boundaries

Imagine this: you're trying to enjoy a Sunday afternoon, a rare moment of tranquility, when suddenly you're reminded of the five tasks you promised you'd complete by tomorrow. The serenity you briefly held slips through your fingers like sand. This is where boundaries come into play, acting as the guardians of your inner peace. Effective boundary-setting doesn't just keep external chaos at bay—it quells the internal conflict that arises when your personal time is under siege by endless commitments. By setting clear boundaries, you create a harmonious space within yourself, a sanctuary where peace and calm reside, shielding you from the stressors that seek to disturb your equilibrium.

Boundaries are the invisible forcefields that reduce internal conflict, allowing you to prioritize what truly matters without the constant tug-of-war between obligations and personal well-being. They help you declutter commitments, focusing your energy on essential tasks that align with your core values. Have you ever felt like a circus performer, juggling flaming torches while riding a unicycle on a tightrope? That's what life feels like without boundaries. By decluttering your commitments, you can step off the tightrope and onto solid ground, where you can breathe and focus on what truly matters.

One of the most effective ways to cultivate inner peace through boundaries is by creating personal rituals for relaxation. These rituals don't have to be elaborate or time-consuming; they simply need to be meaningful to you. It could be as simple as a daily walk in the park, where you let the gentle rustle of leaves soothe your mind, or a quiet cup of tea in the morning before the world wakes up. These moments of intentional peace act as anchors, grounding you amidst the storm of everyday life. By incorporating these rituals into your routine, you're making a commitment to yourself—a promise that your peace is a priority.

Achieving inner peace is not just about the immediate benefits; it's about the long-term transformation that occurs when you consistently uphold your boundaries. Over time, sustained inner peace enhances your overall life satisfaction and boundary resilience. You become more emotionally stable and better equipped to gracefully handle life's ups and downs. It's like building muscle—each time you flex your boundary-setting skills, you strengthen your ability to maintain peace, even when external circumstances threaten to disrupt it. As your inner tranquility grows, so does your ability to set and uphold boundaries, creating a positive feedback loop that supports your well-being.

To truly cultivate inner peace, it's vital to engage in reflective practices that allow you to assess your current state of mind and adjust your boundaries accordingly. Consider keeping a journal where you can explore your thoughts and feelings about your boundaries and the peace they bring you. Reflect on questions like, "What commitments are draining my energy?" or "How can I create more space for relaxation in my life?" These reflective prompts help you stay attuned to your inner needs and inspire you to take action in pursuit of greater peace.

As you prioritize inner peace through boundary-setting, remember that this is not a one-time event but an ongoing process. It's a commitment to yourself, a promise to honor your needs and protect your well-being. By embracing this commitment, you create a life where peace is not an elusive dream but a tangible reality. Boundaries become the framework that supports your tranquility, allowing you to navigate life's challenges with confidence and calm.

In the grand tapestry of life, boundaries are the threads that weave together the fabric of peace. By cultivating inner peace through careful boundary-setting, you lay the foundation for a life where tranquility reigns and stress takes a backseat. As you continue this exploration, you'll find that boundaries are not just lines in the sand but integral aspects of a fulfilling and balanced life. With your newfound insights into emotional resilience, self-care, and mindfulness, you're well-equipped to maintain the peace that boundaries bring. Next, we'll explore communication skills for boundary setting, enhancing your ability to articulate and uphold your needs assertively and confidently.

COMMUNICATION SKILLS FOR BOUNDARY SETTING

I MAGINE THIS: YOU'RE AT a bustling party, the music's loud, and everyone's chatting away. You're trying to enjoy yourself, but your mind's elsewhere. You just remembered agreeing to help a colleague move this weekend—a colleague you barely know. You said yes because you didn't want to seem rude. Now, you're stuck imagining a day of lifting boxes instead of relaxing. If only you'd known how to say no! Welcome to the world of assertive communication, where saying no isn't an act of rebellion but a healthy declaration of your time and energy. Assertive communication is like being the lead dancer in your own life, confidently expressing your needs without stepping on anyone else's toes. It's not about being aggressive; it's about finding that sweet spot where your needs and others coexist peacefully.

Assertive communication is a balanced expression of your needs and rights, crafted and delivered in a way that respects both parties. It's like being a skilled juggler, keeping your needs and the relationship in harmony without dropping a single ball. This balance is crucial because assertive communication contrasts its unruly cousins: aggressive and passive communication. Aggressive communication bulldozes over others, prioritizing your needs at the expense of theirs. It's like a bull in a china shop—destructive and rarely effective. On the other hand, passive communication is like a whisper in a hurricane, often leaving your needs unheard and leading to resentment and stress. Assertive communication, however, finds the middle ground, promoting respect and understanding.

Now, how do you master the art of saying no and still get invited to the next party? It starts with using "I" statements. Try to see it this way: instead of saying, "You always ask me for help when I'm busy," try, "I feel overwhelmed when I add more to my plate." It's a subtle shift, but it changes the focus from blaming to expressing personal limits. This approach not only clarifies your boundaries but also softens the conversation, reducing the likelihood of defensive reactions. And let's talk about the "broken record" technique—one of my personal favorites. It's like that catchy tune you can't get out of your head, but it's your boundary in this case. If someone keeps pushing, calmly repeat your position. "I can't help this weekend. I can't help this weekend." It's firm yet respectful, and eventually, the message sinks in.

But let's be honest—saying no can feel like jumping into a pool of icy water. Guilt and fear of conflict are often lurking in the shadows, ready to pounce. Saying no might conjure images of friends abandoning you or colleagues plotting your downfall. But here's the thing: saying no can actually strengthen relationships. When you set boundaries, you teach others how to respect you and what to expect. It creates a foundation of trust, where both parties understand and honor each other's limits. Remember, every no is a step towards mutual respect and healthier interactions.

To ease the transition into assertiveness, consider practicing through role-playing exercises. It's like a dress rehearsal for life's tricky conversations. Grab a friend—or even a mirror—and simulate a scenario where you need to set a boundary. Whether it's declining a last-minute work project or telling your neighbor you can't dog-sit, these exercises help build confidence. Practicing in a safe, controlled environment reduces anxiety, making real-world applications a breeze. Imagine role-playing a workplace scenario where you need to decline additional tasks. Practicing your response out loud reinforces your assertive language, equipping you with the tools to handle similar situations with poise.

Exercise: Practicing Assertive Communication

Try this role-playing exercise with a friend or in front of a mirror. Scenario: A colleague asks you to cover their shift at the last minute, but you have prior commitments—practice saying no using "I" statements and the "broken record" technique. Reflect on how it feels to assert your needs and adjust your approach as needed.

The Art of Holding Space Without Overcommitting

Picture yourself as a lighthouse—steadfast, guiding without drifting into the stormy seas you illuminate. Holding space is akin to this role, where you offer support and presence to others without getting swept away by their emotional currents. It's about being there for someone, offering a listening ear or a shoulder to lean on while maintaining your own emotional equilibrium. Holding space doesn't mean taking on others' burdens as your own; instead, it's being a compassionate witness to their experiences, allowing them to feel heard and validated without losing yourself in the process. This delicate balance is essential in caregiving roles, where the lines between empathy and overextension can blur all too easily.

Setting boundaries is crucial when holding space for others. Without them, you risk depleting your own emotional resources, leaving you exhausted and unable to support yourself or anyone else. Think of boundaries as the guardrails on a mountain road—they keep you from veering off into dangerous territory. Establishing limits on your time and emotional availability ensures that you can support others without sacrificing your own well-being. It's important to remember that you can't pour from an empty cup; taking care of your needs allows you to be genuinely present for others. This might mean scheduling designated times for checking in with loved ones or setting firm limits on how much emotional energy you're willing to invest in a particular situation.

Balancing empathy and self-care is an art form that requires practice and intention. One effective strategy is practicing active listening without internalizing the emotions being shared. Imagine a friend pouring their heart out over a cup of coffee—your role is to listen and support, not to fix their problems or absorb their distress. By focusing on understanding their perspective without taking it on as your own, you can offer meaningful support while protecting your emotional health. Setting clear intentions before engaging with others can also help maintain this balance. Before a conversation, take a moment to center yourself and clarify your role as a supportive presence rather than a problem-solver. This simple mental shift can prevent you from becoming emotionally entangled in situations that aren't yours to resolve.

Let's take a closer look at a nurse who works in a busy hospital, constantly surrounded by patients in need of care and compassion. Without proper boundaries, the emotional toll of her work could quickly lead to burnout. However, by setting clear limits on her emotional involvement and ensuring she has time for self-care, she can continue to hold space for her patients without sacrificing her own well-being. This might involve taking regular breaks to recharge or engaging in activities outside of work that bring her joy and relaxation. By maintaining these boundaries, she can remain present and empathetic in her role without becoming overwhelmed by the emotional demands of her profession.

Case Study: Successful Boundary-Setting in Caregiving

Meet Sarah, a social worker in a community center. Her job involves supporting individuals facing significant life challenges, often leaving her emotionally drained. Recognizing the need for balance, Sarah implemented a strategy where she scheduled two "quiet hours" each day dedicated to paperwork and reflection, allowing her to recharge. She communicated this boundary to her colleagues and clients, explaining its importance for her effectiveness. This simple yet powerful act of setting aside time for herself enabled Sarah to continue providing compassionate support without compromising her own mental health.

In personal relationships, the same principles apply. Whether you're supporting a friend going through a tough time or a family member in crisis, it's vital to establish boundaries that protect your emotional energy. Remember, you can be a source of comfort and strength without becoming a sponge for others' emotions. Holding space is about being present and empathetic, not about losing yourself in someone else's story. By setting boundaries and practicing self-care, you can continue to be a beacon of support for those around you while maintaining your own well-being.

Navigating Emotional Labor with Clarity

Imagine emotional labor as the unseen effort you put into keeping your emotional mask firmly in place, even when the world around you is falling apart. It's the silent work of managing your feelings and expressions to ensure everyone else remains comfortable and content. In this performance, you're the leading actor, keeping your own emotions tightly choreographed to avoid disrupting the delicate balance of interpersonal interactions. But alas, this is no Broadway show, and unlike a theater performance, there are no intermissions for you to catch your breath. Emotional labor often goes unnoticed, yet it comes with hidden costs that can leave you feeling drained and overwhelmed.

This labor is particularly prevalent in roles where empathy is a job requirement—think customer service representatives who must remain calm and polite, even when dealing with a customer whose volume control seems permanently stuck at eleven. Or take healthcare professionals, who frequently navigate a maze of emotions while tending to patients' needs. Even within the family dynamic, emotional labor is a constant companion. It's the effort of mediating sibling squabbles or managing the emotional temperature of a household during tense family dinners. In these scenarios, you're often expected to suppress your own emotions to keep the peace, resulting in an exhausting balancing act that can leave you emotionally depleted.

So, how do you manage this invisible workload without becoming an emotional pretzel? The answer lies in setting emotional boundaries, the unsung heroes of emotional labor. Just as physical boundaries protect your personal space, emotional boundaries safeguard your mental well-being. They allow you to be present and supportive without getting swept away by the emotional tides of those around you. Establishing these boundaries might mean deciding how much emotional energy you're willing to invest and communicating this clearly to others. For instance, set a limit on how long you'll listen to a friend vent before suggesting a mood-boosting activity. This simple act of setting limits can prevent you from becoming an emotional sponge, absorbing everyone else's stress.

Time management is another trusty tool in your emotional labor toolkit. Balancing emotional labor with other responsibilities requires a strategic approach to your schedule. Allocate specific times for engaging in emotionally demanding tasks, leaving room for activities that recharge your batteries. Just as you wouldn't attempt to run a marathon every day, you shouldn't expect to be emotionally available 24/7. By carving out dedicated time for self-care, you ensure that your emotional resources remain replenished and ready for the next act.

Open communication is key to reducing the burden of emotional labor, yet discussing emotions can feel as awkward as explaining quantum physics to a toddler. Fear not, for scripts can guide the way! Consider approaching conversations with family or colleagues by expressing your emotional needs openly and honestly. Try saying, "I value our relationship and want to be supportive, but I also need some time to recharge so I can be fully present." This conveys your commitment while setting clear boundaries. Being upfront about your emotional limits not only fosters understanding but also encourages others to respect and honor your boundaries.

For parents, the challenge of emotional labor often extends into managing the family's emotional climate. It might involve keeping a smile on your face while refereeing a heated debate over the last slice of pizza or maintaining composure when your teenager insists they know everything about life. In these moments, open communication can be your ally. Share your feelings with your family, explaining that while you're there to support them, you also need moments to recharge. Encourage family members to express their own emotional needs, creating an environment where everyone's feelings are acknowledged and respected.

Navigating emotional labor with clarity requires a blend of self-awareness, communication, and boundary-setting. It's about recognizing your emotional limits and honoring them without guilt. By doing so, you create a space where emotional labor becomes a shared responsibility rather than a solo performance.

Dealing with Energy Vampires

Imagine you're a phone battery in human form, and someone is constantly draining your charge without ever plugging you into the wall. That's an energy vampire for you. These individuals have a knack for sucking the life out of you, leaving you feeling exhausted and overwhelmed. They're not your classic horror movie vampires lurking in the shadows with a cape; instead, they could be friends, family, or colleagues who, intentionally or not, drain your emotional and mental resources. The tricky part is that they often don't come with a warning label, but there are tell-tale signs. Energy vampires frequently exhibit traits like constant negativity, a lack of accountability, and an uncanny ability to turn every conversation back to themselves. They're the ones who, no matter how many times you try to redirect them, always manage to steer the conversation to their drama, leaving you feeling like you've just run a marathon when all you did was sit on a couch.

Recognizing these energy vampires in your life is the first step to reclaiming your vitality. Pay attention to how you feel after interactions. Do you leave conversations feeling drained, stressed, or overwhelmed? If the answer is yes, you might be dealing with an energy vampire. Once identified, the next step is to respond effectively. Setting firm boundaries with these individuals is crucial. It's like putting up a "Do Not Disturb" sign on your emotional door. Be clear about your limits—whether it's how much time you're willing to spend listening to their tales of woe or how often you're available for their venting sessions. Remember, boundaries aren't about pushing people away; they're about protecting your energy so you can be present when it matters most.

Limiting interactions is another strategy to preserve your energy levels. It's not about cutting people out entirely but about managing the time and energy you invest in these relationships. Consider setting specific times for interaction. For instance, if you know a particular friend who tends to call and talk for hours, you might take their calls only when you have the emotional bandwidth to engage. Alternatively, you can suggest meeting in group settings where the energy is more balanced and the focus isn't solely on the energy vampire. These strategies help create a buffer, allowing you to recharge and maintain your well-being.

There are plenty of stories of individuals who've successfully managed interactions with energy vampires. Take, for example, a colleague of mine who had a boss notorious for last-minute demands and endless meetings. Instead of feeling perpetually drained, she set clear boundaries around her availability, politely but firmly communicating her need for advance notice and structured meeting times. By doing so, she was able to protect her energy and perform her job more effectively without succumbing to burnout. Then there's the friend who realized her weekly coffee dates with a particularly needy acquaintance left her feeling exhausted. She shifted these meetings to once a month and found herself with more energy to focus on her own needs and other relationships.

Self-reflection plays a key role in boundary reinforcement, especially when dealing with energy vampires. Regularly assess your energy levels and how interactions impact them. Are you feeling more drained than usual? It might be time to reevaluate your boundaries. Reflective journaling can be an effective tool in this process. Consider prompts like, "What interactions left me feeling energized this week?" or "Where did I feel my boundaries were tested?" This practice helps you stay attuned to your needs and adjust your boundaries accordingly, preventing burnout and fostering emotional resilience.

In this chapter, we've explored the importance of recognizing and managing energy vampires to maintain your well-being. By setting firm boundaries, limiting interactions, and reflecting on your energy levels, you create a protective shield that allows you to navigate relationships with confidence and clarity. These skills will serve as a foundation as we move forward, delving into the nuances of boundary-setting in personal relationships, where maintaining balance and harmony is crucial for nurturing connections and enhancing your overall quality of life.

OVERCOMING FEAR AND GUILT

Overcoming Fear and Guilt

FEAR OF DISAPPROVAL, I'VE found, is like an unwelcome houseguest with a penchant for rearranging your furniture—you don't quite notice the chaos until you trip over the coffee table one too many times. For many of us, the fear of others' judgment is a constant companion, whispering in our ears to play nice, fit in, and keep the peace at any cost. This fear has deep roots, and understanding them is the first step to kicking that pesky guest to the curb. Evolutionarily speaking, being part of the group was crucial for survival; disapproval could mean expulsion, which was a bit of a death sentence back in the day when Wi-Fi didn't exist and saber-toothed tigers were a real problem.

Fast forward to today, and your brain still reacts to disapproval as if a tiger were lurking in your inbox. The amygdala, the brain's alarm system, sounds off, triggering a stress response that makes you feel like you're being chased, even if it's just by a curt email from your boss.

Our desire for acceptance is compounded by social conditioning. We are taught from a young age to seek approval, whether it's through gold stars in school or the number of likes on our latest social media post. When you layer on past experiences of rejection or criticism, the fear of disapproval becomes a finely-tuned symphony of self-doubt. Maybe you remember that time in middle school when you wore that "unique" outfit and the cool kids laughed. That sting of disapproval can linger, shaping our behaviors and making us hesitant to assert our needs or set boundaries. We become people-pleasers, prioritizing others' happiness over our own, often at the expense of our well-being.

Allowing this fear to dictate your actions can lead to a life where your boundaries resemble a sieve more than a fortress. When you prioritize approval over personal needs, you end up saying yes to things that don't serve you, be it extra work projects that eat up your weekends or social events you'd rather skip in favor of a good book and a cup of tea. This can lead to stress, burnout, and a gnawing sense of resentment. Imagine always playing the supporting role in your own life story, where every decision is made to please an audience that may not even be watching. Not only does this compromise your boundaries, but it also chips away at your sense of self-worth and fulfillment.

So, how do we change the script? It begins with challenging the negative beliefs that fuel this fear. Cognitive restructuring is a powerful tool here. Start by identifying the beliefs that hold you back—like the idea that saying no makes you unkind or selfish—and then actively work to replace them with more empowering truths. Visualize positive outcomes where asserting yourself leads to respect and understanding. Picture yourself declining an invitation with grace and the world not ending, but rather your friend nodding in understanding. Practicing these mental exercises can help rewire your brain to see boundary-setting as a strength rather than a flaw.

To bolster this newfound mindset, engage in exercises that build self-confidence. Affirmations that boost confidence are like planting seeds of positivity in your mind's garden. Each morning, look in the mirror and declare, "I am worthy of respect and capable of setting boundaries." It may feel awkward at first, much like dancing in public. Still, over time, these affirmations can transform your internal dialogue. Alongside this, journaling prompts focused on personal achievements can serve as a reminder of your capabilities and resilience. Reflect on moments when you navigated a problematic situation or stood up for yourself—these are the building blocks of confidence.

Exercise: Confidence-Boosting Journaling

Grab a journal and jot down three achievements you're proud of, no matter how small. It could be as simple as speaking up in a meeting or finishing a project ahead of schedule. Then, reflect on how these achievements make you feel and how they contribute to your ability to set and maintain boundaries. Use this exercise as a regular practice to remind yourself of your strength and potential.

By confronting the fear of disapproval head-on, you reclaim your narrative. You shift from seeking external validation to finding it within yourself, empowering you to set boundaries that honor your needs and values.

Transforming Guilt into Empowerment

Guilt is that unwelcome guest who shows up unannounced and eats all your snacks, leaving you to clean up the emotional mess. It often sneaks in when we assert our needs, whispering accusations of selfishness and questioning our self-worth. This pesky emotion is deeply rooted in societal norms that prioritize the happiness of others above our own. From a young age, we're taught to be considerate, which is wonderful, but somewhere along the way, it morphs into an expectation to put others first constantly. This can lead to a life where personal needs are perpetually placed on the back burner, and guilt takes the wheel.

When guilt takes center stage, it can undermine personal autonomy, turning boundary-setting into an uphill battle. Imagine feeling guilty every time you decline an invitation or prioritize your own well-being over someone else's demands. This guilt-induced boundary erosion can leave you feeling as if you're living someone else's life rather than your own. Your time and energy get swept up in a tide of obligations, leaving little room for self-care or personal growth. It's like building a sandcastle too close to the waterline—beautiful but constantly threatened by the incoming tide. Over time, the erosion of boundaries can lead to burnout and resentment as you realize you're living according to others' expectations rather than your own desires.

But guilt doesn't have to be the villain in your story. With a little reframing, it can become a catalyst for empowerment. Start by viewing guilt as a signal rather than a verdict. Instead of allowing it to dictate your actions, use it as information—a clue that there's a misalignment between your actions and values. For instance, if you feel guilty about spending a day off by yourself, ask yourself why. Does it stem from a belief that your worth is tied to productivity, or perhaps from the notion that you must always be available to others? By identifying these underlying beliefs, you can begin to challenge and reframe them.

Engaging in self-reflection exercises can help you pinpoint where guilt is unjustified. Set aside time to reflect on instances where guilt has influenced your decisions. Ask yourself whether the guilt stems from external pressures or internalized beliefs that no longer serve you. Once you've identified these patterns, work on developing a guilt-to-growth action plan. This plan involves setting intentional boundaries that align with your values and gradually increasing your comfort with asserting them. For example, if you often feel guilty about saying no to social events, start small by declining one invitation a month and observing the outcome. Use these experiences to build confidence in your ability to prioritize your needs without guilt.

Transforming guilt into empowerment also involves recognizing the positive aspects of setting boundaries. Each time you assert your needs, you reinforce your self-worth and honor your autonomy. Put yourself in the shoes of Emma, who always felt guilty about leaving work on time, thinking she should stay late to help her colleagues. By realizing that her guilt was rooted in an unrealistic expectation of self-sacrifice, Emma began setting boundaries around her work hours. Over time, she found that not only did her productivity improve, but her colleagues respected her more for maintaining a healthy work-life balance. Emma's experience illustrates how reframing guilt can lead to personal empowerment and healthier relationships.

Exercise: Guilt-to-Growth Action Plan

Take a moment to develop your own guilt-to-growth action plan. Identify a specific situation where guilt often arises, and reflect on the beliefs fueling this guilt. Write down one small boundary you can set to challenge these beliefs, and commit to practicing this boundary in the coming weeks. Keep track of your feelings and any positive changes you notice. Use this exercise as a stepping stone to transform guilt into a motivator for growth and empowerment.

By embracing guilt's transformative potential, you can reclaim your autonomy and set boundaries that reflect your true self.

Handling Conflict with Confidence

Ah, conflict—the delightful spice of life that nobody ordered but everyone seems to get served. It's like that extra side of jalapeños on your nachos when you specifically asked for mild. Setting boundaries can sometimes feel like you're donning a suit of armor, ready to fend off dragons, when in reality, you're just trying to keep your weekend free from unsolicited dog-sitting requests. But let's face it: conflict is a natural part of any relationship. It's not the end of the world; it's simply two people seeing things from different angles. Think of conflict as a dance—sometimes you step on toes, but eventually, you find your rhythm. When boundaries come into play, conflicts often arise because boundaries are essentially you saying, "This is where my needs stand, and I'd appreciate it if you didn't trample them." Such statements can ruffle feathers but are vital for maintaining healthy interactions.

Yet, the mere thought of conflict can send shivers down our spines. Many of us dread it like a Monday morning alarm, fearing that confronting boundary issues might damage relationships beyond repair. We worry that a simple "no" could unravel years of friendship or camaraderie. Confrontation has earned a bad rap, primarily because we associate it with aggression and hostility. But what if I told you that conflict, when handled well, can actually strengthen relationships? It's true. Addressing issues head-on, rather than sweeping them under the rug, builds trust and understanding. It's like cleaning out the cobwebs in your attic—messy at first but ultimately refreshing and rewarding.

So, how do you navigate these turbulent waters without capsizing? It starts with honing your active listening skills. This means truly hearing what the other person is saying, not just waiting for your turn to talk. Imagine a conversation where you genuinely tune in to someone's concerns, nodding and acknowledging their feelings before diving into your perspective. By doing this, you defuse tension and create a space for open dialogue. Think of active listening as the WD-40 in your relationship toolkit—it lubricates the gears of communication, making everything run more smoothly.

Another effective strategy is nonviolent communication, a tool that can transform potentially explosive conversations into constructive exchanges. This technique involves expressing your feelings and needs without blame or judgment. It's about saying, "I feel overwhelmed when..." rather than "You always make me feel overwhelmed." By focusing on your own experiences, you avoid triggering defensiveness in others, creating a space where both parties can express themselves honestly. Nonviolent communication is like being a diplomat at the United Nations of your personal life—negotiating peace treaties rather than declaring war.

Take, for example, the story of a colleague who constantly felt overburdened by her team's last-minute demands. Instead of harboring resentment, she decided to address the issue head-on. She scheduled a meeting with her team and used nonviolent communication to express her feelings: "I've been feeling a lot of stress when projects are handed to me at the last minute. I'd love to find a way to plan better together." Her team responded positively and worked out a schedule that respected everyone's time. This approach not only resolved the immediate issue but also improved team dynamics and productivity.

In a family setting, imagine a parent who struggles with their teenager's habit of borrowing things without asking. Instead of letting frustration simmer, the parent might sit down with their child and say, "I feel disrespected when my belongings are taken without permission. Can we agree on a system to ask first?" By framing the conversation around their feelings and needs, they open the door to a solution that honors both parties. This type of conflict resolution is like finding a shared melody in the cacophony of daily life—bringing harmony where there was once discord.

As you navigate the complexities of conflict and boundaries, remember that every conversation is an opportunity for growth and connection. Embrace conflict as a chance to deepen your understanding of yourself and others. In doing so, you cultivate relationships that are resilient, authentic, and deeply rewarding.

The Role of Self-Compassion in Boundary-Setting

Self-compassion, in many ways, is like that supportive friend who always has your back, offering kindness and understanding no matter how messy things get. It's the ability to treat yourself with the same gentleness and care that you would extend to a dear friend who just spilled coffee on their white shirt right before a big meeting. Self-compassion is crucial in the realm of boundary-setting because, let's be honest, it isn't always a walk in the park. Differentiating self-compassion from self-indulgence is essential here. Whereas self-indulgence might involve binge-watching an entire season of a show while ignoring pressing deadlines, self-compassion encourages you to acknowledge your struggles without judgment, treating yourself with kindness as you navigate the challenges of maintaining boundaries.

Incorporating self-compassion into your life can work wonders for overcoming emotional barriers that often accompany boundary-setting. It acts like a balm, soothing the sting of rejection or the guilt that sometimes arises after saying no. By reducing self-criticism, self-compassion allows you to approach boundary-setting with a mindset of growth and resilience. Imagine the relief of not beating yourself up for needing a break, instead recognizing it as a natural part of self-care. Embracing self-compassion also boosts emotional resilience, providing the strength to withstand the discomfort that can accompany asserting your needs. It's like having a sturdy umbrella during a storm, protecting you from the downpour of self-doubt and external pressures.

Developing self-compassion isn't just about thinking pleasant thoughts; it involves actionable practices that can be woven into your daily routine. One effective technique is mindful self-compassion exercises, which encourage you to become aware of your thoughts and feelings without judgment. This might involve taking a few moments each day to sit quietly, noticing your breath, and gently acknowledging any emotions that arise. It's about observing your inner landscape with curiosity rather than criticism. Another powerful practice is loving-kindness meditation, where you focus on sending positive intentions to yourself and others. Picture yourself enveloped in a warm, glowing light, extending love and acceptance to every part of your being. These exercises are like planting seeds of self-love that grow into a garden of resilience and strength.

Stories of transformation through self-compassion abound, illustrating its profound impact on boundary-setting. There's an interesting bit about Jake, a young professional who always struggled with saying no at work, fearing he'd disappoint his boss. By incorporating self-compassion into his life, Jake began to recognize his tendency to overcommit as a response to his harsh self-judgment. Through mindful self-compassion practices, he learned to appreciate his efforts and set realistic boundaries without guilt. This shift allowed him to confidently communicate his limits, resulting in a healthier work-life balance and improved relationships with colleagues. Then there's Mia, a parent who often felt guilty for taking time for herself amid the demands of family life. Embracing self-compassion helped Mia see that her well-being was essential for her family's happiness, leading her to set boundaries around self-care time—and the world didn't end!

As we draw this chapter to a close, remember that self-compassion is a powerful ally in the boundary-setting process. By treating yourself with kindness and understanding, you create a foundation for resilience and empowerment, allowing your boundaries to flourish. In the next chapter, we'll explore how to apply these principles to nurturing personal relationships, ensuring that connections with loved ones are both fulfilling and respectful.

BOUNDARIES IN PERSONAL RELATIONSHIPS

S TEP INTO THIS STORY for a second: you're at a family dinner, surrounded by loved ones when suddenly Aunt Mabel asks when you're going to settle down and have kids. Cue the awkward silence as you frantically search your brain for a polite reply that doesn't involve flipping the table and moving to a remote island. Family dynamics can be a minefield of well-intentioned yet intrusive questions, unsolicited advice, and the occasional guilt trip that would shame even the most dramatic soap opera. Welcome to the world of family boundaries, where finding harmony between closeness and independence is like navigating a winding river in a canoe, trying to avoid both crashing into the banks and drifting off course. In families, boundaries are essential for protecting your well-being and maintaining a sense of self, much like how a sturdy fence keeps nosy neighbors from peering into your living room.

Boundaries in family dynamics are crucial for ensuring that relationships remain healthy and fulfilling. They act as protective barriers that allow you to engage with your family without losing sight of your individuality. Imagine boundaries as your personal superhero, swooping in to save the day whenever Aunt Mabel's curiosity turns into an interrogation. In parent-child relationships, boundaries help maintain respect and foster independence. It's about ensuring that while you love your parents dearly, you're not calling them to ask what to wear to a meeting (unless, of course, it's a fashion-themed intervention). Setting boundaries is like planting a garden; you need to create a space where each plant—be it parent or child—can grow without overshadowing the other.

Managing expectations from extended family can be a delicate dance. While family gatherings can evoke a mix of joy and tension, they often come with a side of unsolicited advice and questions about your life choices. Over-involvement in personal decisions by family members can lead to boundary issues, leaving you feeling like your life is an open book for everyone to read, critique, and rewrite. It's like having a committee of editors for every chapter of your life story, each with their own opinion on how the plot should unfold. These challenges can make it difficult to maintain personal autonomy and assert your needs without feeling guilty or misunderstood.

So, how do you assert boundaries with your family without starting World War III? It begins with setting clear expectations during family interactions. This involves communicating your needs openly and honestly, much like explaining to Aunt Mabel why you're not ready to discuss your five-year plan over mashed potatoes. Assertive communication is your best friend here. It's about expressing your personal limits in a way that's respectful yet firm. Instead of saying, "Stop asking me about kids," try, "I appreciate your concern, but I'd rather focus on the present." It's a subtle shift, but it transforms potential conflict into a dialogue that respects both parties' perspectives.

Reflecting on your personal values and family roles can also guide your boundary-setting efforts. Understanding your role within the family and how it influences your boundaries is key to maintaining balance. Are you the peacemaker, constantly smoothing things over to keep the harmony? Or perhaps you're the trailblazer, forging your path while others watch from the sidelines, popcorn in hand. Recognizing these roles can help you identify where your boundaries may need reinforcement. Journaling is an excellent tool for this reflection. Consider prompts like, "What values are most important to me in my family relationships?" or "How does my role in the family impact my boundary-setting?" These exercises encourage introspection, providing clarity on where adjustments are needed to align your boundaries with your values.

Journaling Prompt: Assessing Family Roles and Values

Take a moment to reflect on your role within your family. Consider how this role influences your boundaries and interactions. Write about a specific family interaction where you felt your boundaries were tested. What values were at play, and how might you adjust your approach to align with your values?

Incorporating these strategies into your family interactions can help you maintain the delicate balance between closeness and independence. Remember, boundaries aren't about shutting family out; they're about creating a space where everyone's needs are respected and valued.

Healthy Boundaries in Romantic Relationships

Ah, romance—the domain where butterflies flutter, hearts race, and boundaries are sometimes as elusive as unicorns. In a world where love songs often preach the mantra of "giving everything to the other person," it can be easy to forget that healthy relationships thrive on mutual respect, understanding, and, yes, boundaries. Imagine boundaries as the scaffolding that supports the relationship structure, allowing it to stand tall and weather the storms. They are the unsung heroes that foster mutual respect by ensuring each partner's needs, desires, and limits are acknowledged and honored. When boundaries are in place, partners can engage in open, honest communication, reducing misunderstandings and increasing relationship satisfaction. It's like having a compass in an unfamiliar forest—it guides your path, makes the journey less daunting, and helps you avoid wandering aimlessly in circles.

Recognizing when boundaries are being violated in a romantic relationship is crucial to maintaining its health. Subtle signs of boundary violations can creep in, like uninvited guests at a wedding, disrupting the harmony. Controlling or manipulative behaviors, such as dictating who you can see or what you can wear, are glaring red flags. These behaviors might be masked as concern or love, but they are often rooted in insecurity and a desire for control. It's like being wrapped in a warm blanket that slowly turns into a straitjacket. Other signs include guilt-tripping, where one partner makes the other feel bad for asserting their needs, or constant criticism disguised as "constructive feedback." If you notice these patterns, it's time to hit the pause button and reassess the situation.

Establishing and maintaining boundaries with your partner doesn't have to be a Herculean task. It starts with honest conversations, where both partners openly discuss their needs and expectations. Regular check-ins are a fantastic way to keep the boundary lines clear and flexible. Consider setting aside time each month to sit down with your partner and discuss what's working and what's not. Think of it as relationship maintenance—like how you wouldn't drive a car for years without an oil change. These check-ins create a safe space for both partners to express concerns and adjust boundaries as needed. Additionally, agreeing on personal space and time is vital. Whether it's a solo Saturday morning run or a weekly night out with friends, having time apart can actually bring you closer together, much like the old saying, "Absence makes the heart grow fonder."

Real-life stories illuminate the power of boundary negotiation in romantic relationships. Take, for instance, a couple I know—let's call them Alex and Jamie. They found themselves constantly bickering over household chores, each feeling the other wasn't contributing enough. Instead of allowing resentment to fester, they decided to sit down and openly discuss their expectations. They created a shared responsibility chart, assigning tasks based on preference and availability. Over time, this small act of boundary-setting transformed their relationship, reducing tension and increasing their appreciation for each other's contributions. Then there's the story of Mia and Chris, who struggled with differing social needs. While Mia loved hosting parties, Chris preferred quiet nights in. Through candid discussions, they agreed to balance their social calendar, ensuring both partners felt comfortable and respected. These examples highlight how effective boundary negotiation can foster harmony and understanding, turning potential points of conflict into opportunities for growth.

In romantic relationships, boundaries are like the rhythm that keeps the dance of love in step. They create a balance where both partners can feel secure and valued without losing their individuality. By recognizing the importance of boundaries, identifying violations, and establishing clear communication, you lay the groundwork for a relationship that is resilient, fulfilling, and deeply connected.

Friendship Dynamics: When to Say No

Friendships are the playground of our adult lives, offering laughter, support, and the occasional late-night ice cream binge. But just like any playground, they need rules to keep things fun and safe. Enter boundaries, the unsung heroes of healthy friendships. Setting boundaries is vital because they protect your personal time and energy, ensuring you don't end up as your friend's personal therapist, dog sitter, and emotional punching bag all rolled into one. Boundaries allow you to keep your cup full, so you can actually enjoy those Friday night hangouts instead of dreading the inevitable midnight call about their latest existential crisis.

Friendship boundary-setting can be like walking a tightrope. On one side, you have the fear of hurting your friend's feelings; on the other, the risk of being overwhelmed by their needs. Friends who demand excessive emotional support can quickly become the emotional equivalent of a black hole, sucking in all your energy and leaving you feeling like a deflated balloon. These situations often arise when one friend is going through a tough time. While it's natural to want to help, it's crucial to recognize when your support is turning into a one-way street. It's like offering someone a ride only to realize you've become their full-time chauffeur without ever being asked.

Learning to say no in friendships is an art form; like all art, it requires practice. It's about mastering the ability to decline requests without turning the friendship into a soap opera. Start by practicing empathy while asserting your personal limits. You can acknowledge your friend's needs while expressing your own, much like saying, "I know you're going through a lot and I care about you, but I need some time to recharge." This approach balances compassion with self-care, ensuring you don't sacrifice your well-being on the altar of friendship.

Humor is another powerful tool for setting boundaries. It can diffuse tension and make the process of saying no feel less like a confrontation and more like a friendly banter. See if this resonates: your friend invites you to a last-minute camping trip, but you've already planned a weekend of binge-watching Netflix while relaxing on your couch. Instead of a flat "no," try something like, "As much as I'd love to wrestle with mosquitoes and questionable campfire cuisine, my couch and I have a hot date this weekend." It's light-hearted, straightforward, and shows you value your time without offending your friend.

Reflecting on friendship dynamics and personal needs is crucial for maintaining balance. It's about taking a step back and evaluating whether your friendships align with your values and needs. Are there friendships that leave you feeling drained rather than uplifted? Are you always the one giving while your needs take a backseat? Journaling can be a helpful tool in this reflection process. Consider prompts like, "What qualities do I value most in a friendship?" or "How do I feel after spending time with my friends?" Writing these reflections down can offer clarity and reveal areas where boundaries may need reinforcement.

Friendships are meant to be mutually beneficial, a dance of give and take where both parties feel valued and supported. By setting boundaries, you ensure that this dance remains harmonious, with each partner moving in sync rather than stepping on each other's toes. Remember, saying no doesn't make you a bad friend; it makes you a wise one. It allows you to show up fully for your friends without losing yourself in the process.

Setting Boundaries During Family Gatherings

Ah, family gatherings—a time for joy, laughter, and the occasional unsolicited critique of your life choices. Here's a story to bring this to life: you're at the annual holiday dinner, trying to enjoy your mashed potatoes in peace, when suddenly, you're bombarded with questions about your career, relationship status, and why you haven't taken up Aunt Edna's suggestion to try goat yoga yet. These gatherings can be delightful, but they also come with their own sets of challenges, particularly when it comes to maintaining boundaries. There's a unique pressure to conform to familial expectations, often leaving you feeling like a contestant on a game show where the grand prize is a heaping dose of guilt. It's no wonder many of us find these events mentally and emotionally taxing.

One of the most common challenges at family gatherings is managing unsolicited advice or criticism. You know the kind—the well-meaning but often intrusive suggestions that make you wonder if you should have pursued a degree in diplomacy instead of whatever you actually do. Navigating these interactions requires a blend of tact and assertiveness. It's about mastering the delicate art of nodding politely while internally rolling your eyes. One strategy is preparing responses to common boundary violations. Practice phrases like, "I appreciate your concern, but I'm happy with my current choices," or "Thanks for the suggestion, but I've got this covered." These responses acknowledge the input without committing to follow it, preserving your autonomy while keeping the peace.

Establishing time limits for interactions is another useful approach. It's perfectly acceptable to set boundaries on how long you'll engage in certain conversations, especially those that tend to veer into uncomfortable territory. Consider employing a "conversation timer"—a mental note to switch topics after a set amount of time. If Aunt Edna starts her annual monologue on the benefits of goat yoga, you might decide to steer the conversation towards more neutral topics like the weather or the latest episode of a popular TV show. This technique helps maintain your boundaries while keeping the mood light and friendly.

Self-care before and after family gatherings is crucial for maintaining your well-being. Think of it as your pre- and post-game routine. Before the event, engaging in mindfulness exercises can help you enter the gathering with a calm and centered mindset. Simple practices like deep breathing or a short meditation can reduce anxiety and prepare you for whatever comes your way. Visualize yourself setting and maintaining boundaries with ease, like a seasoned diplomat at a peace summit. After the gathering, take time to reflect and recharge. This might involve journaling about your experiences, focusing on what went well, and identifying areas for improvement. Engage in relaxation techniques, such as a hot bath or a gentle yoga session, to release any lingering tension and restore your mental and emotional equilibrium.

Let me share a story from one of my holiday gatherings. I remember dreading the inevitable barrage of questions about my career trajectory from relatives I hadn't seen in a year. So, I decided to prepare a mental list of topics to redirect the conversation, like my latest travel adventures or a new hobby I'd picked up. As expected, the questions came but equipped with my trusty list; I navigated them like a pro. "You're still in the same job?" was met with, "Yes, but I recently learned to play the ukulele!" It not only shifted the focus but also sparked genuine interest and laughter, making the experience enjoyable for everyone. This small act of boundary-setting transformed what could have been an uncomfortable exchange into a memorable moment of connection.

As we wrap up our exploration of boundaries in personal relationships, remember that setting and maintaining boundaries is a powerful act of self-care and respect. Whether with family, friends, or romantic partners, these boundaries create a space where everyone can thrive. They are the foundation of healthy, fulfilling relationships, allowing you to engage with others while honoring your own needs. In our next chapter, we'll delve into the professional realm, exploring how to navigate workplace dynamics with the same grace and assertiveness you've cultivated here.

Boundaries in Professional Settings

Here's a scenario that might help: It's a typical Tuesday morning, and you're at your desk with a cup of coffee that's more milk than caffeine, ready to tackle your to-do list. Suddenly, your boss swings by with a grin that can only mean one thing—more work. As they casually mention a "quick project" that needs your attention, you find yourself nodding along, even as your inner voice screams, "Noooo!" Fast forward a few weeks, and you're buried under a mountain of tasks, your weekends have become an endangered species, and burnout is looming on the horizon like a villain in a melodrama. This, my friends, is why setting boundaries at work is not just a nice-to-have but an absolute must for career longevity and personal health. Professional boundaries act as a buffer against the relentless demands of the workplace, ensuring that you can sustain your efforts without sacrificing your sanity.

Overcommitting at work can feel like signing up for an all-you-can-eat buffet when you're already full. It might seem manageable at first, but before you know it, you're overwhelmed and exhausted. Burnout is the sneaky consequence of consistently saying yes when you mean no, and it can lead to a cascade of negative effects—from decreased productivity to the dreaded Sunday Scaries. The American Psychological Association notes that a whopping 79% of U.S. workers experience job stress, often due to excessive workload and inadequate work-life balance. When you constantly overextend yourself, you're not only compromising your health but also your career prospects. After all, a burnout-riddled employee is much like a car running on empty—eventually, something's going to give.

The fear of saying no at work is a common plight among employees, akin to a universal rite of passage. There's the anxiety of missing out on opportunities, the dread of damaging relationships with colleagues, and the nagging worry of being perceived as uncooperative. You might fear that by setting limits, you'll be passed over for promotions or exciting projects. It's a bit like walking a tightrope in a business suit, trying to balance assertiveness with diplomacy. Yet it's essential to remember that saying no doesn't mean you're not a team player; it means you're strategically managing your workload to deliver quality results. The real trick lies in how you communicate your boundaries without burning bridges.

To navigate this delicate dance, it's crucial to develop the art of declining requests professionally. Imagine you're a diplomat negotiating a treaty rather than a gladiator in the Colosseum. One effective strategy is to frame refusals with constructive feedback. For example, if a colleague asks you to take on additional tasks during a busy period, you might say, "I'm currently focused on X project, which is at a critical stage. Perhaps we can revisit this request once it's completed?" This way, you're not just saying no but offering a rationale and a potential solution. It's like serving a slice of humble pie with a dollop of understanding on the side.

Another key to maintaining professional relationships is using assertive language to communicate your capacity limits. Assertive communication involves clearly and respectfully stating your needs while considering others' feelings. It's about finding that sweet spot between being a pushover and a bulldozer. "I" statements are your best friend in this scenario. If someone asks you to work late, try saying, "I need to leave at my scheduled time today to meet other commitments. Can we discuss prioritizing this task during my work hours?" You're asserting your boundary while maintaining a positive tone, akin to a firm yet gentle handshake.

To put these strategies into practice, consider these common workplace scenarios. Scenario one: A colleague asks you to review their presentation slides at the last minute. Your response could be, "I'd love to help, but I'm currently tied up with another deadline. Could we arrange a time tomorrow to go over them together?" Scenario two: Your boss assigns you a new project when you're already swamped. You might say, "I'm excited about this new project and want to give it my best. Could we prioritize it alongside my current workload to ensure quality delivery?" These scripts provide a framework for maintaining boundaries without sacrificing your professional relationships or credibility.

Exercise: Practicing Assertive Communication at Work

Try this exercise: Think of a recent situation at work where you felt overwhelmed by requests. Write down your ideal assertive response using the techniques discussed—framing refusals with constructive feedback and utilizing "I" statements. Practice this response out loud, adjusting your tone and language as needed.

Incorporating these techniques into your professional repertoire equips you with the tools to say no without fear. By setting boundaries, you're not just protecting your time and energy; you're investing in your career by ensuring that you remain engaged, productive, and fulfilled.

Managing Workplace Stress Through Boundaries

Imagine, if you will, a day at the office where your to-do list is as long as a CVS receipt. You're juggling endless emails, back-to-back meetings, and a boss who loves the phrase "urgent deadline" a bit too much. By the time you get home, you're more fried than the onions on your burger. This is stress, my friend, and it's a sneaky little gremlin that can wreak havoc on both your productivity and mental health. When stress goes unmanaged, it's like trying to run a marathon while carrying a backpack full of bricks—inevitably, something's got to give. You may find yourself calling in sick more often, not because you've caught the latest bug, but because your body's saying, "Enough!" Productivity takes a nosedive, errors creep into your work, and your usual sparkle dims into a dull flicker.

A significant factor contributing to workplace stress is the lack of clear boundaries. It's like being a goalie without a net—everything's coming at you, and there's no way to block the shots. Often, stress stems from overlapping roles and undefined job responsibilities, leaving you to play a game of professional pinball, bouncing from task to task without clear direction. Additionally, the constant connectivity courtesy of our beloved smartphones means you're reachable 24/7. Your work might as well be a clingy partner, always demanding more of your attention, even when you're trying to unwind. This expectation of constant availability can blur the lines between work and personal life, making it difficult to switch off and recharge.

But fear not, for there are strategies to reclaim control and set boundaries that can alleviate stress. First, let's talk about setting clear priorities and communicating them effectively with your manager. It's like being the captain of your own ship, deciding what cargo to keep and what to toss overboard. By identifying your key tasks and priorities, you can focus your energy on what truly matters, reducing the feeling of being pulled in a million directions. Once you've established these priorities, communicate them with your manager. A simple, "I'm currently focused on X and Y, which are aligned with our project goals. Could we revisit Z next week?" can work wonders in managing expectations and workload.

Another powerful technique is allocating specific times for checking emails and messages. Picture yourself as a secret agent on a mission: you wouldn't answer every call or text during a high-stakes operation, right? The same logic applies here. By designating certain times for communication—say, twice a day—you can concentrate on your tasks without constant interruptions. This not only boosts productivity but also creates a mental boundary between work and personal life, allowing you to relax without the nagging thought of unread emails.

Let's look at an example of effective boundary-setting in action. Meet Claire, a manager at a bustling tech company. Claire found herself drowning in emails and requests, her workload more bloated than a post-Thanksgiving belly. Realizing the toll it was taking on her health and performance, she decided to delegate tasks more effectively. By clearly defining roles within her team and empowering her colleagues to take ownership of their projects, Claire lightened her load and reduced stress. The result? A happier, more productive team and a manager who could finally enjoy her evenings without work looming over her like a storm cloud.

The key takeaway here is that boundaries are not about erecting walls but about creating a framework that supports your well-being. They act as a compass, guiding your actions and decisions in a way that aligns with your values and goals. By implementing these boundary-setting strategies, you can reduce workplace stress, enhance your performance, and reclaim your peace of mind. So, grab that metaphorical compass and start charting a course towards a more balanced, less stressful work life.

Protecting Personal Time in a Professional Environment

Let's face it—personal time is like that elusive sock that always seems to vanish from the laundry. Just when you think you've got a handle on it, work sneaks in and swipes it away. Yet, maintaining personal time is crucial for your mental and emotional health, much like oxygen is to, well, breathing. It's the downtime that recharges your batteries, keeps burnout at bay, and allows you to show up as your best self at work and home. Work-life balance isn't just a buzzword; it's the tightrope that prevents you from plunging into the abyss of exhaustion. Without personal time, even the most motivated among us can find ourselves staring blankly at our computer screens, wondering whether we've accidentally become part of a corporate hamster wheel.

In the hustle and bustle of modern work life, it's easy to let personal time slip through the cracks, especially when workplace norms subtly encourage it to do so. The expectation to be available after hours is a prime culprit. It's as if the office has a giant, invisible vacuum cleaner that sucks you back in, even when you're supposed to be off the clock. Emails ping in at all hours, and there's an unspoken rule that responding quickly is the key to professional sainthood. Then there's the unpaid overtime that somehow becomes a regular feature on your weekend calendar, transforming your two-day respite into an extension of your workweek. It's like a magician's trick, only you're the one pulling a disappearing act on your free time.

So, how do you reclaim your personal time and guard it like a prized possession? Start by setting specific work hours and communicating them clearly. Think of it as drawing a line in the sand, one that says, "Beyond this point, work shall not pass." Whether you're a 9-to-5er or working flexible hours, make it known when you're on the clock and when you're off. Make use of your email's auto-reply feature to inform colleagues of your availability, setting the expectation that you won't respond outside of these hours. It's like putting up a "Do Not Disturb" sign on your digital doorstep, and it works wonders for maintaining boundaries.

Scheduling regular personal breaks and vacations is another key strategy. These aren't just luxuries; they're necessities for maintaining your well-being. Pencil in short breaks during your workday to step away, stretch, and breathe. Consider them mini-vacations that refresh your mind and boost your productivity. When it comes to actual vacations, don't just let them accumulate like unused gym memberships—take them! Disconnect from work emails and let yourself truly unwind. You'll return with renewed energy and a fresh perspective, ready to tackle challenges with gusto.

So, there's this story about Tom, an employee at a bustling marketing firm who found himself drowning in work commitments. Tom negotiated flexible work hours with his manager, explaining that a slight shift in his schedule would allow him to balance his workload with personal responsibilities. By starting his day an hour earlier, he created a buffer in the afternoon to dedicate to activities he enjoyed, like running or spending time with his family. This small adjustment made a world of difference, improving his focus and well-being while maintaining his productivity.

Reclaiming personal time in a professional environment isn't about shirking responsibility; it's about setting boundaries that allow you to thrive both personally and professionally. By establishing clear work hours and taking regular breaks, you create a framework that supports your holistic well-being. Take a page from Tom's book and explore how you can negotiate flexible arrangements that suit your lifestyle. Your personal time is valuable, and safeguarding it ensures you bring your best self to every aspect of your life.

Navigating Boundaries in Remote Work Settings

The allure of remote work is undeniable. You get to swap the morning commute for a leisurely stroll to your home office (or kitchen table) and trade the corporate dress code for something more comfy—like pajamas. But this setup comes with its own set of challenges, especially when it comes to setting boundaries. The line between work and home life blurs faster than an ice cream cone on a hot day. Suddenly, the temptation to work beyond regular hours creeps in, and before you know it, you're sending emails at midnight while your cat stares at you, questioning your life choices.

One of the biggest boundary issues remote workers face is the lack of physical separation between work and personal spaces. Your home office might double as your dining room, and the laptop that once symbolized freedom now feels like a ball and chain. Add to this the difficulty in disconnecting from work-related technology, and you've got a recipe for burnout. Notifications ping relentlessly, each one a siren call pulling you back into work mode when you should be unwinding with a good book or binge-watching your favorite series. It's a bit like having a boss who never leaves, constantly hovering over your shoulder.

Setting boundaries in a remote work environment requires intention and creativity. Start by creating a dedicated workspace that signals to your brain, "This is where work happens." Even if it's just a small desk in the corner, having a designated area can help draw that crucial line between work and home life. Think of it as marking your territory—not with anything unsavory, but perhaps with a nice plant or a motivational poster. This space becomes your command center, a place where you can switch into work mode and, just as importantly, switch out of it at the end of the day.

Establishing a clear start and end to your workday is another powerful strategy. Without a commute to bookend your day, it's easy to let work hours spill over into personal time, like an overenthusiastic puppy. Set a defined time for beginning and ending your work, and stick to it as if your sanity depends on it—because it just might. Simple acts like closing your laptop or shutting down your computer can serve as physical reminders that the workday is over. These rituals help create a mental boundary, allowing you to transition from professional to personal life with ease.

Step into the world of Alex, a graphic designer who found himself working around the clock when his home became his office. The absence of a clear work schedule led to late nights and frazzled days. Realizing the impact on his well-being, Alex decided to implement time-blocking techniques. He designated specific hours for work tasks, creative brainstorming, and client meetings, building in buffer periods for breaks and personal activities. By compartmentalizing his time, Alex regained control over his schedule and found a healthy balance between work and leisure. This approach not only improved his productivity but also enriched his personal life, allowing him to enjoy hobbies and quality time with loved ones.

Navigating boundaries in remote work settings is about reclaiming control over your environment and schedule. By creating a dedicated workspace and establishing a clear start and end to your workday, you can prevent work from seeping into every corner of your life. These strategies empower you to maintain a healthy balance, ensuring that remote work remains a blessing rather than a curse. As we move forward, remember that setting boundaries is an ongoing process. It's not about getting it perfect from the start, but about making adjustments that support your well-being and personal growth.

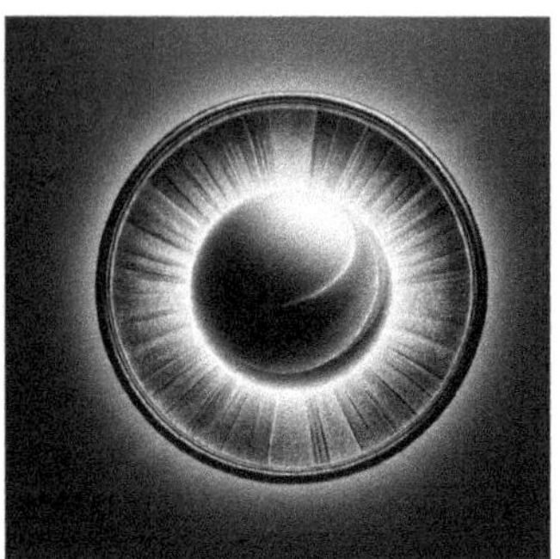

BOUNDARIES FOR EMPATHS AND PEOPLE PLEASERS

L ET'S PAINT A MENTAL picture: You're at a party, juggling a conversation about cryptocurrency with a stranger and simultaneously reassuring your friend that, yes, their ex's new haircut does look like a ferret. You're exhausted, yet here you are, nodding along, absorbing everyone's emotions like you're some kind of human sponge. Sound familiar? Welcome to the world of empaths and people pleasers, where emotional overload is as common as misplaced socks in a laundry basket. You might find yourself constantly caught in a whirlwind of other people's emotions, feeling their joy, their sorrow, and even their Monday morning blues. It's like being on an emotional rollercoaster, except you didn't buy a ticket, and the operator looks suspiciously like your Aunt Martha.

Empaths and people pleasers often experience emotional overload, a state where your emotional reserves are as depleted as your willpower during a holiday sale. But how do you know when you've hit that point? The signs are there, if you're willing to take a moment to listen to your body and mind. Chronic fatigue and exhaustion are key indicators that your boundaries have been compromised. It's like your body is waving a white flag, begging for a nap and a Netflix marathon. You might also notice heightened anxiety and irritability, where even the sound of a chirping bird can make you want to channel your inner grump. These symptoms are your body's way of saying, "Hey, we need a break from this emotional buffet."

The causes of emotional overload are as varied as a buffet table, but two main culprits often stand out: excessive empathy and the inability to say no. Over-identifying with others' emotions can turn you into an emotional sponge, soaking up feelings like a paper towel in a soda spill. While it's a beautiful gift to be empathetic, it can also lead to feeling overwhelmed and disconnected from your own emotions. Lack of personal downtime and reflection exacerbates the situation, leaving little room to recharge or connect with yourself. Without these moments of solitude, it's easy to lose track of where others' emotions end and yours begin.

But fear not, dear reader, for there are ways to mitigate emotional overload before it leaves you feeling like a deflated balloon at a birthday party. Start with regular emotional check-ins, where you take a moment to pause and assess how you're feeling. It's like giving your emotions a roll call, ensuring everyone is present and accounted for. Setting daily limits on emotional engagement is another powerful tool. Think of it as putting a cap on your emotional bandwidth, much like limiting your data usage to avoid overage charges. By consciously choosing when and how to engage, you preserve your emotional energy for what truly matters.

Emotional boundaries play a critical role in maintaining balance and preventing overload. They act as the gatekeepers of your emotional well-being, differentiating between support and personal responsibility. Imagine being a lifeguard at an emotional pool, where your job is to ensure everyone stays afloat without jumping in and drowning yourself. It's important to remember that while you can offer support, you're not responsible for rescuing everyone from their emotional depths. Recognizing what is yours to carry and what belongs to others allows you to maintain a healthy distance while still offering compassion and empathy.

Exercise: Emotional Check-In Chart

Create a simple chart to track your emotional state throughout the day. Divide the chart into time slots (morning, afternoon, evening) and jot down a quick note about how you're feeling during each period. This exercise helps you become more aware of your emotional shifts and identify any patterns of overload. Use this awareness to adjust your boundaries and prioritize self-care activities as needed.

In the world of empaths and people pleasers, setting emotional boundaries is akin to building a sturdy dam to control the flood of emotions that can overwhelm you. By recognizing the signs of emotional overload, understanding its causes, and implementing strategies to manage it, you equip yourself with the tools to navigate this complex landscape.

Strategies for Balancing Compassion and Self-Care

Balancing compassion and self-care is like trying to hold a yoga pose while juggling oranges—challenging but not impossible. Compassion is that warm, fuzzy feeling that makes you want to help others, like when you see a kitten stuck in a tree and immediately start planning a rescue mission. But if you're not careful, too much compassion can leave you feeling like an empty cup, with not a drop left for yourself. Enter self-care, the superhero of boundaries. It's not just bubble baths and face masks, though those are delightful. Self-care is about replenishing your energy reserves so you can continue to offer genuine compassion without running on fumes. The synergy between self-care and empathetic interactions is a beautiful dance, where each step you take to care for yourself enhances your ability to be there for others. It's like refilling your own cup before pouring into someone else's. By prioritizing self-care, you ensure that your compassion is sustainable, not a one-time burst of energy.

To maintain this delicate balance, it's vital to schedule regular self-care activities. Think of self-care as an appointment with your best self, and yes, it's perfectly okay to write it in your planner with the same importance as that meeting with your boss. Whether it's a morning walk to clear your mind, a yoga session to stretch away the stress, or a quiet evening with a book that doesn't require any emotional investment, these activities are the fuel that keeps your engine running smoothly. It's about consciously carving out time in your day to recharge, like plugging in your phone every night so it's ready for the next day. Another key strategy is setting clear intentions before offering help. This means pausing for a moment to assess your own emotional state before diving into someone else's crisis. Ask yourself, "Do I have the energy and emotional space to offer support right now?" It's like checking the weather before deciding to wear flip-flops or boots. By being intentional, you ensure that your compassion comes from a place of abundance, not obligation.

Maintaining a balance between compassion and self-care leads to healthier relationships and a more sustainable caregiving role. When you care for yourself, you build emotional resilience—a sort of psychological armor that protects you from emotional burnout. You're less likely to feel overwhelmed by others' needs and more capable of offering support without losing yourself in the process. This balance also enhances empathy, allowing you to connect with others more deeply and authentically. It's like having a well-tuned instrument that plays beautiful music without the strings snapping. Feel the weight of the situation with Jamie, a dedicated caregiver who discovered the power of balancing compassion with self-care. For years, Jamie put others first, often working double shifts to support her patients but neglecting her own needs. It wasn't until a close friend introduced her to the concept of self-care that Jamie realized she couldn't pour from an empty cup. She began incorporating small acts of self-care into her daily routine—like taking a quiet walk during her lunch break or spending ten minutes meditating before bed. These changes, though subtle, transformed her approach to caregiving. Jamie found herself more present and patient with her patients, able to offer genuine empathy without feeling drained. Her relationships improved, and she discovered a newfound passion for her work, fueled by the balance she had achieved.

As a parent juggling the demands of family life, I've learned that setting boundaries and prioritizing self-care is not just a luxury; it's a necessity. It's like putting on your own oxygen mask first so you can help others. When you're stretched too thin, your ability to offer compassion is compromised, and you risk burnout. By embracing self-care as an integral part of your life, you create a foundation for genuine compassion and meaningful connections.

Shielding Yourself from Emotional Drains

Ever felt like your emotional battery is on low and the universe forgot to include a charger? You're not alone. Empaths and people pleasers often find themselves drained by their surroundings, much like that phone that always seems to be dying at the worst possible moment. Emotional drains come in many forms, from toxic relationships that suck the joy out of the room to high-stress environments that make you want to hide under the covers with a do-not-disturb sign. These situations can turn your emotional world into a chaotic carnival ride, with manipulative individuals as the creepy clowns who never seem to leave. Whether it's a colleague who thrives on drama or a friend who calls only when they need a shoulder to cry on, these drains leave you feeling like you've run a marathon without the benefit of endorphins.

High-stress environments are another culprit—those relentless pressure cookers filled with demanding social situations and constant noise. Picture yourself in a crowded room, the chatter a deafening buzz, each conversation a potential energy thief. It's like trying to read a book in the middle of Times Square. These environments can zap your emotional energy faster than a toddler on a sugar high. And let's not forget about the media that bombards you with emotionally charged content, leaving you feeling as if the weight of the world is perched on your shoulders.

So, how do you protect yourself from these emotional vampires? Start by establishing firm boundaries with toxic individuals. It's like building a moat around your emotional castle, only without the pesky maintenance. Be clear about what behaviors you won't tolerate and stick to your guns, even if it means saying no to that friend who always needs a last-minute favor. Reducing exposure to emotionally draining media is another essential step. Consider setting specific times to check the news or social media, ensuring you're not constantly absorbing the world's woes. It's like putting a time lock on your emotional pantry, only opening it when you're ready to digest what's inside.

Energy management is crucial for maintaining well-being and building resilience. It's about knowing where your energy goes and making sure you save some for yourself. Prioritize activities that replenish your energy, like a walk in the park, a quiet cup of tea, or a guilty pleasure TV show that requires zero brainpower. These activities act as a recharge station for your soul, filling you up so you can face the world with a full tank.

To reinforce your emotional boundaries, try visualization techniques. Imagine an emotional shield surrounding you, deflecting negativity and keeping your energy intact. Picture it as a bubble of calm, bouncing off stressors like a superhero's force field. Another tool is daily affirmations, reminding yourself of your worth and the importance of personal boundaries. Say it out loud: "My energy is precious, and I choose where to spend it." It's like a daily reminder post-it for your mind, keeping your boundaries front and center.

Exercise: Visualization and Affirmation Practice

Every morning, take five minutes to visualize your emotional shield. Close your eyes and imagine a protective bubble enveloping you, repelling negativity and stress. Pair this with an affirmation, such as, "I am in control of my energy. I am worthy of peace." Repeat this affirmation three times, letting it sink in like a soothing balm. Use this practice to strengthen your emotional defenses, ensuring that you face the day with confidence and clarity.

In a world filled with emotional drains, it's important to be your own guardian, choosing what to let in and what to keep out. By recognizing the sources of emotional depletion and implementing strategies to protect yourself, you create a sanctuary of calm amidst the chaos. Remember, your energy is your own, and you have the power to decide where it flows.

Embracing Authenticity Without Overcommitment

Living authentically is like wearing your favorite pair of shoes—not only do they fit perfectly, but they make you feel like you can conquer the world. For empaths and people pleasers, authenticity is the secret sauce that adds flavor to life, allowing you to set boundaries that reflect who you truly are. When your actions align with your personal values, you stop living someone else's script and start writing your own. Authenticity gives you the freedom to be yourself, without the burden of trying to fit into molds that just don't fit. It's the difference between living in a house of mirrors, where you're constantly reflecting others' expectations, and living in a home where every room is decorated to your taste. Yet, maintaining authenticity without overcommitting can feel like walking a tightrope, with the pressure to conform acting as a gusty wind trying to tip you off balance. The world often expects you to meet its demands, whether it's attending every social event or agreeing to every favor asked. There's a fear of missing out, a nagging voice that insists you'll be left behind if you don't say yes to every opportunity. This pressure can lead to a life where your calendar is full, but your heart feels empty.

To embrace authenticity while setting boundaries, it's crucial to practice mindful decision-making. This means pausing before committing to anything and asking yourself, "Does this align with my values and priorities?" It's like having a mental checklist that helps you decide whether to RSVP with a yes or a polite decline. Establishing criteria for which commitments to accept is another helpful strategy. Imagine you're curating an art gallery, and you're selective about what pieces make the cut. Your time and energy are your masterpieces, meant to be shared with care. Cast your mind to the story of Alex, an empath who was always the first to volunteer for every project at work, even when it meant late nights and missed weekends. One day, Alex decided enough was enough and started evaluating each request against his personal values: Was this project meaningful to him? Would it contribute to his long-term goals? By doing so, Alex began to set boundaries that honored his authenticity, resulting in a work-life balance that allowed him to thrive.

Similarly, consider Emily, a people pleaser who found herself saying yes to every social invitation, leaving her weekends jam-packed with events she didn't really enjoy. Emily started by identifying her core values, such as spending quality time with close friends and nurturing her love for painting. She then used these values as a guide to decide which invitations to accept, learning to say no to those that didn't bring her joy or align with her priorities. This shift allowed Emily to embrace her true self, leading to more meaningful connections and a renewed sense of fulfillment.

Embracing authenticity while setting boundaries is about being true to yourself, even when the world tries to pull you in different directions. It's about knowing that you're not obligated to meet every demand placed on you and that your worth isn't measured by how much you can give. Authenticity is your compass, guiding you to create a life that resonates with your values and aspirations. As you navigate the challenges of authenticity and boundary-setting, remember that it's okay to prioritize your needs and that doing so allows you to offer your best self to the world.

In the next chapter, we'll explore how boundaries can be a powerful tool for healing, helping you reclaim your autonomy and rebuild your sense of self after experiencing codependency or trauma. As you continue this exploration, know that each step you take towards setting boundaries is a step toward living a life that truly reflects who you are and what you stand for.

HEALING FROM CODEPENDENCY AND TRAUMA

YOU KNOW THAT MOMENT when you look in the mirror and don't quite recognize the person staring back at you? It's like seeing a ghost of who you used to be, and you can't help but wonder, "How did I get here?" Trauma and codependency have a sneaky way of blurring the reflection, making it hard to see where you end and the rest of the world begins. It's as if you're wearing someone else's glasses, and everything is just a bit out of focus. These experiences can erode your sense of self, leaving you feeling like a supporting character in your own life story. The repeated violation of boundaries can chip away at your self-concept, creating a distorted view of who you are. It's like being a marshmallow left too close to the campfire, slowly losing shape and form until you're a gooey mess.

Rebuilding self-identity through boundaries is like finding your way back home after being lost in the woods. Boundaries act as the trail markers that guide you back to yourself, helping you rediscover and affirm your true essence. They allow you to establish personal values and preferences, much like a painter selecting the colors for their masterpiece. With boundaries, you differentiate between self and others in decision-making, ensuring your needs are prioritized without guilt or hesitation. It's about putting yourself back in the driver's seat of your life, steering toward the destinations that matter most to you. By setting and maintaining boundaries, you create a framework that supports your journey of self-discovery and growth.

The process of rebuilding self-identity is deeply personal, yet incredibly rewarding. It begins with self-reflection, a practice that allows you to peel back the layers and reconnect with your core values. Journaling is a powerful tool in this process, offering a space to explore questions like, "What do I truly value?" and "What brings me joy?" These prompts help you identify the guiding principles that shape your identity. Creating a vision board is another effective exercise, providing a visual representation of your aspirations and the life you wish to cultivate. It's like crafting a blueprint for your future, where each image and word reflects a piece of your authentic self. By engaging in these activities, you gain clarity on who you are and what you stand for, paving the way for meaningful boundary-setting.

Exercise: Vision Board for Self-Identity

Gather magazines, photos, and any other materials that resonate with you. Find a quiet space and create a vision board that represents your core values, aspirations, and the life you want to build. Let your intuition guide you as you select images and words that align with your true self. Display your vision board in a place you'll see daily, serving as a reminder of your journey to rediscover and affirm your identity.

A strong self-identity is the bedrock of effective boundary-setting. When you're clear about who you are and what you value, you're more confident in asserting your needs and standing firm in your decisions. This increased confidence acts as a shield, protecting you from the pressures and expectations of others. It empowers you to enforce boundaries consistently, much like a lighthouse guiding ships safely to shore. With a solid sense of self, you navigate life's challenges with resilience, knowing that your boundaries are not barriers, but bridges to a life that reflects your true essence.

In the grand scheme of things, rebuilding your self-identity is about reclaiming your narrative and living life on your terms. It's about recognizing that you are the protagonist of your story, and you hold the pen that writes each chapter. As you explore and affirm your identity, you gain the strength to set boundaries that honor your values and aspirations. This process is transformative, allowing you to step into your power and embrace a life of authenticity and fulfillment.

Breaking Free from Codependency Patterns

Codependency is like being tied together in a three-legged race, except you didn't sign up for it, and the other person keeps tripping you up. It's an imbalanced relationship dynamic where personal boundaries become as blurry as a Monet painting. You find yourself deeply enmeshed with someone else, where your sense of self is wrapped around their needs and emotions. This creates a cycle of dependency and control, where one person often assumes a caretaker role, and the other becomes reliant, knowingly or unknowingly. It's like being on a seesaw with someone who refuses to get off, leaving you in a perpetual state of imbalance and unease.

Recognizing the signs of codependency in your relationships is like spotting a plot twist in a movie you've seen a thousand times. You might notice an over-investment in others' problems, where you're more concerned about solving their issues than managing your own. It's like being a superhero in your own mind, but instead of wearing a cape, you're wearing yourself thin. Another telltale sign is the inability to express your own needs. You might find yourself nodding along to plans you don't agree with or swallowing your words to avoid conflict.

It's as if your voice is on mute, and you're watching someone else narrate your life.

Breaking free from these patterns requires a conscious effort to establish healthier relational dynamics. The first step is to develop assertive communication skills. Think of this as upgrading from a dial-up connection to high-speed internet, where your needs and thoughts can finally be expressed clearly and confidently. Practice using "I" statements, which shift the focus from blame to personal experience, like saying, "I feel overwhelmed when I take on too much," rather than, "You always make me do everything." This subtle shift empowers you to communicate your boundaries without igniting defensive reactions.

Self-care and self-reliance are your allies in this transformation. Picture self-care as your personal toolkit, stocked with everything from bubble baths to boundary-setting pep talks. By prioritizing your well-being and spending time alone, you rebuild your sense of independence, much like a phoenix rising from the ashes. Self-reliance involves setting goals and engaging in activities that fulfill you, not just the ones that please others. It's about finding joy in your own company and realizing that you don't need someone else to complete you.

Stories of triumph over codependency can be both inspiring and relatable. Take, for example, Lisa, who spent years in a relationship where her partner's needs always took precedence. Lisa decided to set boundaries by first identifying her own needs and then communicating them openly. She started small, like designating an hour each day for her hobbies, and gradually expanded her boundaries to include more significant aspects of her life. Over time, Lisa transitioned to an interdependent relationship, where mutual respect and support became the foundation, rather than obligation and control.

Similarly, consider Tom, who realized his friendships were draining him because he constantly prioritized others' crises over his own peace. Tom began practicing self-care by setting aside weekends to recharge and focus on his interests. He communicated this boundary to his friends, explaining that while he valued their friendship, he needed time for himself to maintain balance. This shift allowed Tom to foster mutual respect in his relationships, where support became a two-way street rather than a one-way toll road.

These success stories illustrate that breaking free from codependency is not only possible but also incredibly liberating. By setting boundaries and nurturing your self-reliance, you create relationships that are balanced and fulfilling. You regain the freedom to be yourself, unapologetically and without reservation.

Establishing Autonomy After Trauma

Imagine trauma as a thief in the night, stealthily swiping your autonomy and leaving you feeling like a passenger in your own life. It's as though someone else is dictating your every move, while you sit in the backseat, silently yearning for the steering wheel. Traumatic experiences can shatter the illusion of control, making helplessness your unwanted companion. In this state, your sense of self-agency may dissolve, as if you've forgotten how to lead your life. It's a bit like finding your favorite pair of shoes missing and having to tiptoe through a world of uncertainty. This loss of autonomy can lead to feelings of vulnerability and disorientation, where even the simplest decisions feel out of reach.

Setting boundaries becomes an empowering way to reclaim your autonomy. They serve as the scaffolding upon which you rebuild your sense of self-determination. Boundaries create safe spaces for personal growth, much like planting a garden in a fortified courtyard. Within this protected area, you can nurture your aspirations without fear of intrusion. These boundaries are your personal guardrails, helping you navigate life while avoiding the potholes of stress and triggers. Imagine setting limits on the time you spend in environments that exacerbate anxiety, allowing you to gradually expand your comfort zone. By creating these spaces, you construct a haven where your autonomy can flourish, free from the shadows of trauma.

To establish autonomy post-trauma, practical techniques are your trusted allies. Goal-setting exercises can illuminate your path, much like a trail of breadcrumbs leading you back to your center. Start by defining your personal aspirations, breaking them down into achievable steps. Think about the dreams that ignite your passion, and chart a course that aligns with your values. This process not only clarifies your direction but also empowers you to take ownership of your choices. Building a support network is another invaluable strategy. Enlist allies who encourage your growth and hold you accountable. It's like creating a safety net, ensuring that even when you stumble, you have a cushion to catch you.

The transformation from victim to empowered individual is a journey marked by resilience. Let's unpack the events that transpired with Jane, who once felt trapped by her past experiences. She began setting boundaries, starting small—like choosing how much time she spent with certain people. Over time, these actions built her confidence, allowing her to reclaim her life. Jane's narrative illustrates the power of boundaries in fostering empowerment and resilience. As she moved from a place of fear to a position of strength, she discovered that her autonomy was not lost, merely misplaced.

These personal growth narratives are beacons of hope, illuminating the path from helplessness to empowerment. They remind us that boundaries are not just lines drawn in the sand; they are bridges to a life where you hold the reins. Through consistent boundary-setting, you gain the courage to step into your power, embracing a future where your choices are guided by your aspirations, not your fears.

In the grand tapestry of life, boundaries are the threads that weave autonomy back into your narrative. They empower you to write your own story, one where you are not defined by trauma but by the strength you cultivate in its aftermath. Embracing boundaries as tools of empowerment allows you to take the wheel and steer your life in the direction of your choosing. As you continue on this path, remember that each boundary you establish is a testament to your resilience, a declaration that your autonomy is yours to reclaim.

Boundaries as a Tool for Emotional Safety

Emotional safety is like having a cozy blanket for your mind, wrapping you up in a sense of protection and ease. It's about creating a personal space where your mental and emotional well-being can thrive, even amid life's chaos. Boundaries play a crucial role in this process. They act as the invisible lines that define what is acceptable in your interactions and relationships, ensuring that you don't end up feeling like a doormat at a muddy festival. Healthy emotional spaces are nurturing and respectful, where your boundaries are acknowledged and upheld. Unhealthy ones, however, can feel like trying to hold a picnic during a hurricane, leaving you exposed and vulnerable. Differentiating between these spaces is key to maintaining emotional safety.

Threats to emotional safety can lurk in various corners of your life, like un-invited guests at a party you didn't plan. Toxic relationships and environments are prime culprits, often characterized by manipulation, control, and disrespect. Whether it's a friend who constantly criticizes you or a workplace that thrives on drama, these situations can erode your emotional well-being. Emotional manipulation and gaslighting are particularly insidious threats, where someone might twist your words or make you doubt your reality. It's like being in a funhouse of distorted mirrors, where nothing is as it seems, and you're left questioning your sanity. Recognizing these threats is the first step in protecting your emotional space.

Setting boundaries is your best defense against these emotional intrusions. Start by setting limits on emotional disclosure, deciding what, when, and with whom you share your feelings. It's like having a guest list for your inner world, where only trusted individuals get an invite. This doesn't mean you have to become a fortress of solitude, but rather that you choose wisely who gets to enter your emotional circle. Creating and enforcing personal rules for interaction is another powerful strategy. These rules might include walking away from conversations that become toxic or refusing to engage in arguments that go in circles. It's about drawing a line in the sand and saying, "This is where I stand, and I won't be budged."

This reminds me of something that happened to Emily, who found herself constantly drained by a friend who treated her more like a therapist than an equal. Emily decided to set boundaries by limiting their conversations to lighter topics and gently steering away from discussions that left her feeling depleted. This change not only protected Emily's emotional well-being but also im-proved the quality of their friendship, allowing for more balanced and enjoyable interactions. Similarly, in a high-stress work environment, Jack realized that gossip and negativity were sapping his energy. He set boundaries by avoiding certain conversations and focusing on positive interactions with colleagues who uplifted him. These small, intentional changes created a safer emotional space for both Emily and Jack, allowing them to navigate their relationships with confidence and clarity.

Achieving emotional safety through boundaries isn't just about avoiding harm; it's about fostering environments where you can flourish. By setting and upholding boundaries, you create a sanctuary for your emotional health, free from the chaos and negativity that threaten to destabilize it. As you become more adept at identifying and managing these threats, you'll find yourself better equipped to handle life's emotional rollercoasters without losing your balance. Boundaries become the safety harness that secures you, allowing you to enjoy the ride with confidence and peace.

In weaving boundaries into the fabric of your life, you construct a tapestry of emotional safety that supports and nurtures you. This chapter has explored the power of boundaries in creating spaces where you can thrive, free from the shadows of past experiences. As you continue to embrace the role of boundaries in your life, you'll discover newfound strength and resilience, ready to face whatever challenges lie ahead. Let these insights guide you as you move forward, one boundary at a time.

INTEGRATING BOUNDARIES INTO DAILY LIFE

I MAGINE YOUR LIFE AS a grand theatrical production. In this play, you're not just the star but also the director, stage manager, and sometimes even the understudy. Now, picture boundaries as the script that keeps the drama from turning into a chaotic improvisation. Without them, you'd be ad-libbing your way through every scene, trying to remember your lines while dodging the spotlight's glare. Integrating boundaries into daily life is akin to rehearsing your lines until they become second nature. This chapter is about establishing daily rituals that reinforce your boundaries, helping you maintain the balance between the spotlight and the shadows.

One of the most powerful rituals you can adopt is setting daily intentions each morning. Think of it as a gentle nudge that guides your day, much like the subtle notes a director might give before a big performance. As you sip your morning coffee, take a moment to visualize the boundaries you need to uphold throughout the day. Whether that's saying no to a colleague's request or ensuring you have time to recharge, these intentions act as your internal compass, pointing you toward a day of balanced interactions. By establishing this morning ritual, you set the stage for a day where your boundaries are clear and respected, allowing you to move through the world with confidence and ease.

Evening reflections are another vital component of boundary maintenance. As you wind down for the night, take a few minutes to evaluate your day's boundary triumphs and challenges. Imagine this as a post-performance review, where you assess what went well and where improvements can be made. Did you manage to uphold your boundaries during a difficult conversation, or did you find yourself agreeing to something you didn't want to do? Reflecting on these moments helps reinforce your boundary intentions and build resilience for the future. It's a chance to celebrate your victories and learn from any missteps, ensuring that your boundaries remain strong and adaptable.

Structured routines are the backbone of effective boundary-setting, much like a precisely choreographed dance that reduces the risk of stepping on toes. Consistency in daily practices helps reduce decision fatigue, allowing you to focus your energy on maintaining your boundaries rather than constantly reinventing the wheel. Just as dancers rely on muscle memory to execute complex routines, daily rituals create mental muscle memory that supports your boundary goals. This consistency not only reduces stress but also enhances your ability to navigate life's demands with clarity and purpose.

One practical suggestion for integrating boundary-focused activities into your daily life is gratitude journaling. By taking a few moments each day to jot down what you're grateful for, you reinforce positive boundaries and cultivate a mindset of abundance. Gratitude journaling acts as a mirror that reflects the goodness in your life, grounding you in appreciation and helping you maintain perspective. Another effective ritual is incorporating mindful pauses during transitions between activities. These pauses act as brief intermissions that allow you to recalibrate your focus and energy, ensuring that you approach each task with intention and presence.

Personalization is key when it comes to boundary rituals, as no two people's boundary scripts are identical. Much like tailoring a costume to fit the unique contours of an actor, your rituals should reflect your individual needs and lifestyle. Create a personalized boundary mantra—a phrase or affirmation that encapsulates your boundary intentions and serves as a constant reminder. This mantra can be as simple as "I honor my needs" or "My boundaries are my strength." Additionally, consider designing a boundary vision board, a visual representation of your boundary goals and aspirations. This board serves as a daily reminder of the life you're creating, empowering you to uphold your boundaries with authenticity and conviction.

Interactive Exercise: Creating Your Boundary Vision Board

Take a moment to gather materials for your boundary vision board. This can include magazines, photographs, quotes, or any other visual elements that resonate with your boundary aspirations. Spend some time arranging these items on a board or a digital platform, crafting a visual representation of the boundaries you wish to uphold. As you engage in this creative process, reflect on the emotions and intentions each element evokes. Place your completed vision board in a space where you'll see it daily, allowing it to inspire and motivate you to maintain your boundaries with confidence and grace.

As you personalize these rituals, remember that they are not rigid scripts but flexible guidelines that evolve with you. Just as a director might tweak a scene to fit a new interpretation, your rituals can adapt to the changing dynamics of your life. The goal is to create a routine that feels authentic and empowering, supporting you as you navigate the complexities of daily life with boundaries that uplift and protect you.

Using Technology to Support Boundary Goals

Here's a way to see it: you're sitting at your desk, surrounded by a sea of digital devices, each vying for your attention with an incessant parade of pings, dings, and alerts. It's like being in a never-ending game of digital whack-a-mole, where every notification is a new mole popping up to steal your focus. Technology can be both a blessing and a curse when it comes to setting boundaries. On one hand, it offers tools that can help you precisely maintain boundaries. On the other, it has a sneaky way of creeping into every nook and cranny of your life, making it hard to know where your time went.

But don't despair—technology can actually be your greatest ally in maintaining boundaries if you know how to wield it wisely. Let's start with digital reminders. These little nudges can be lifesavers in a fast-paced world. Imagine setting a reminder on your phone to take a five-minute stretch break every couple of hours. It's like having a personal assistant who gently taps you on the shoulder and says, "Hey, don't forget to breathe." These breaks are crucial for maintaining your mental well-being and ensuring you don't burn out by the time the clock strikes noon.

Focus and productivity apps are another technological boon for boundary maintenance. They act like digital bodyguards, helping you fend off distractions and keep your attention on the task at hand. Apps like Forest, Focus@Will, and brain.FM, for instance, are designed to help you concentrate by minimizing interruptions and enhancing your focus with music or virtual trees. By carving out dedicated time for work or personal projects, these apps help you create mental space that's free from digital clutter.

Of course, the key to using technology effectively is setting clear limits. It's all too easy to fall down the rabbit hole of endless scrolling or binge-watching, only to emerge hours later wondering where your day went. To prevent this, establish screen time limits for yourself. Most smartphones now offer built-in tools that track your usage and alert you when you're approaching your daily limit. Consider them your friendly digital watchdogs, reminding you to put the device down and step back into the real world.

Social media detox periods can also be transformative. These are times when you intentionally unplug from social media to recharge and reconnect with yourself. It might feel odd at first like you've suddenly lost an appendage, but the peace and clarity that come from disconnecting are worth it. Use this time to engage in activities that restore your energy, whether it's reading, hiking, or simply enjoying a quiet cup of tea.

Let's look at a real-life example of technology-enhanced boundary practices. Meet Emily, a busy professional who found herself constantly overwhelmed by work emails flooding her inbox at all hours. She decided to use calendar apps to block out personal time and prioritize work tasks. By setting specific periods for checking and responding to emails, she created a boundary that allowed her to focus on deep work without distractions. Emily also scheduled "tech-free" evenings, where she silenced her phone and focused on family time, hobbies, and self-care. The result? Emily felt more in control of her time and energy, with her boundaries firmly in place.

In our technology-driven world, the challenge isn't just about managing devices; it's about managing how they impact our lives. It's easy to let technology dictate our schedules and invade our personal space, but with intentionality, it can become a powerful tool for boundary-setting. By harnessing digital reminders, focus apps, screen time limits, and social media detoxes, you can reclaim your time and maintain a sense of balance. Technology can be your ally in creating a life where boundaries support your well-being instead of being hurdles you constantly have to jump over.

Scheduling Self-Care as a Non-Negotiable

Imagine yourself in this moment: your friend invites you to a weekend getaway, but you've already promised yourself a solo date with your favorite book, a bubble bath, and perhaps a cheeky snack or two. Self-care is often the first thing to get booted off our calendars when life gets busy. Yet, ironically, it's the very thing that keeps us from turning into a frazzled mess. Treating self-care as a scheduled, non-negotiable activity is like putting on your superhero cape—it equips you to face the world with a bit more sanity and a lot less stress. When you carve out dedicated time for self-care, you reinforce your boundaries, reminding yourself and others that your well-being is a top priority.

Now, you might be thinking, "How on earth do I fit self-care into my already jam-packed schedule?" The secret lies in scheduling it with the same seriousness as a dentist appointment or a work meeting. Imagine blocking out time on your calendar for a yoga class or a leisurely walk as though it were a business meeting with your most important client—yourself. By treating self-care with this level of importance, you ensure it doesn't get pushed aside in favor of other demands. Creating a self-care checklist can also be a game-changer. Jot down small, manageable activities that bring you joy and relaxation, and tick them off as you go. It's incredibly satisfying to see your self-care achievements accumulate, like a collection of happy little victories.

The benefits of consistently prioritizing self-care go far beyond a temporary mood lift. When you make self-care a regular part of your routine, you tap into a wellspring of increased energy and focus. It's a bit like recharging your phone overnight; you wake up each day with a full battery, ready to tackle whatever challenges come your way. This renewed vitality makes it easier to maintain your boundaries, as you have the mental and emotional resources to assert your needs without hesitation. Moreover, self-care fosters resilience, allowing you to bounce back from setbacks with grace and confidence. It's like building a reserve of inner strength that you can draw upon whenever life throws you a curveball.

Take Sarah, for example. A busy mother of two and a part-time yoga instructor, she used to feel like she was constantly running on fumes. Her days were a blur of school drop-offs, work commitments, and household chores, leaving little time for herself. Determined to make a change, Sarah started scheduling 30-minute self-care sessions three times a week. Whether it was a yoga session, a quiet coffee break, or simply sitting in her garden, these moments became her sanctuary. Over time, Sarah noticed she had more energy and patience, both at work and at home. Her boundaries became more apparent, and she found it easier to say no to additional commitments that didn't align with her priorities. Sarah's experience illustrates the transformative power of self-care when it is treated as a non-negotiable part of daily life.

Incorporating self-care into your routine doesn't have to be a grand affair. It's about finding small pockets of time and filling them with activities that nourish your body and mind. Whether it's a quick meditation session during your lunch break or a relaxing bath before bed, these moments act like mini-vacations, giving you the space to unwind and recharge. It's important to remember that self-care looks different for everyone. What rejuvenates one person might not work for another, so exploring various activities and finding what resonates with you is essential. The goal is to create a self-care routine that feels authentic and sustainable, supporting your overall well-being and boundary resilience.

As you embark on this journey of prioritizing self-care, embrace it with humor and an open mind. Allow yourself to enjoy the process, knowing that each act of self-care is a declaration of your worth and an investment in your long-term happiness. Whether it's painting your nails, practicing mindfulness, or simply taking a moment to breathe deeply, these small acts of kindness towards yourself add up, creating a foundation of well-being that supports you in all areas of life. So go ahead, block out that time, and make self-care your non-negotiable. Your future self will thank you.

Creating a Supportive Environment for Boundaries

Imagine you're trying to bake a cake, but your kitchen is a chaotic mess—flour everywhere, pots clanging, and your toddler deciding that now's the perfect time to practice their drum solo on your pans. Not exactly conducive to a stress-free baking experience, right? The same principle applies to setting boundaries: your environment—both physical and social—plays a significant role in how well you can maintain them. When your surroundings align with your personal values and needs, they become an ally in your boundary-setting efforts, much like a well-organized kitchen makes baking a breeze.

Creating a boundary-supportive environment begins with decluttering spaces to minimize distractions. Think of it as a mental spring cleaning, where you remove the unnecessary noise so you can focus on what truly matters. Maintaining an orderly environment helps reduce stress and supports concentration, whether in your workspace or living room. By tidying up your physical space, you create a sanctuary that promotes relaxation and focus, allowing you to uphold your boundaries with greater ease.

But it's not just about the physical environment; the people you surround yourself with matter just as much. Building a network of supportive relationships is like having your own personal cheerleading squad ready to bolster your boundary goals. These are the people who understand and respect your need for boundaries and who don't take offense when you decline an invitation or need some alone time. They're the ones who remind you that it's okay to put yourself first and who encourage you to stick to your commitments, even when it's challenging.

To transform your environment into a boundary-friendly space, consider redesigning your workspaces to enhance concentration. This might mean setting up a dedicated desk area with minimal distractions, using noise-canceling headphones, or even introducing a few plants to bring a sense of calm to your surroundings. At home, create spaces that encourage relaxation and rejuvenation. Find a corner of your home where you can unwind, whether it's a cozy reading nook or a serene spot for meditation. By consciously designing these areas, you signal to yourself—and others—that your boundaries are non-negotiable.

Let's take a look at a family that successfully created a supportive environment for boundaries. The Smiths, a family of four, found that their household was a whirlwind of activities, with everyone pulling in different directions. To address this, they implemented household boundary agreements. Each family member sat down to discuss their individual needs and expectations, from quiet study time to screen-free dinners. By establishing these boundaries together, they created a home environment that respected each person's space and time. The result was a more harmonious household where each member felt heard and valued, with clear boundaries that supported their personal well-being.

Creating a supportive environment for boundaries isn't about making drastic changes overnight. It's about incremental shifts that align your surroundings with your goals. It requires an honest assessment of what aspects of your environment enhance your boundary-setting efforts and which ones hinder them. As you modify your spaces and relationships, you'll find that maintaining boundaries becomes less of a struggle and more of a natural extension of your daily life. Remember, your environment is a reflection of your commitment to yourself, a testament to the boundaries you've set to honor your needs and aspirations.

ADVANCED BOUNDARY-SETTING TECHNIQUES

YOU KNOW WHEN YOU'RE at a buffet, plate in hand, and you realize that the sheer variety of options is both a blessing and a curse? That's what life feels like when you're trying to set boundaries. Each area of our lives—work, family, friends—has its own flavor, and trying to apply the same boundary-setting approach to all of them is like using the same sauce for every dish. Spoiler alert: it doesn't work. Instead, think of boundary-setting as a custom-made suit tailored to fit the unique contours of each situation. This chapter is all about creating those bespoke boundaries that fit perfectly, no matter where you wear them.

Customizing boundaries is essential because, let's face it, life is not a one-size-fits-all affair. What works for your work life might not cut it with your family, where the dynamics are as predictable as a toddler on a sugar rush. At work, you should set boundaries around your availability, ensuring that your email doesn't turn into a 24/7 hotline. Here, it's vital to establish specific hours for work-related communications, much like putting your phone on do-not-disturb mode. However, in family settings, boundaries might revolve around the emotional support you can offer without draining yourself dry. This means learning to say, "I need some me-time," without feeling like you've committed a capital offense.

Assessing your boundary needs in diverse situations is like conducting a personal needs assessment, and it's worth taking the time to reflect on what triggers require a boundary adjustment. Maybe it's that monthly meeting that feels like a scene from a horror movie or a family gathering that leaves you feeling more drained than a marathon. Identifying these triggers is the first step to tailoring your boundaries. Once you've pinpointed what's throwing you off balance, you can create a plan to address it. Consider jotting down the times when you feel your boundaries are being stretched too thin. This record becomes your guide, helping you see patterns and act accordingly.

Techniques for customizing boundaries are as varied as the situations they address. A flexible boundary framework is your best friend here. This framework is like a Swiss Army knife, adaptable to your context. For instance, you might decide that you're open to impromptu meetings at work, but only if you've had your morning coffee. In family settings, you might be perfectly willing to host gatherings, but you draw the line at cleaning up after everyone leaves. Adjusting your boundaries based on feedback and reflection is key. Think of it as a GPS recalculating your route when you take a wrong turn.

Take the case of Maria, a globetrotting consultant who needed to adapt her boundaries to different countries and cultures. In some places, work-life balance was a priority, so she had to enforce strict boundaries around her availability after hours. In others, the culture valued extended family involvement, requiring her to balance professional obligations with familial commitments. By customizing her boundaries, Maria was able to maintain her sanity and effectiveness, whether she was in New York or New Delhi.

Interactive Exercise: Personal Needs Assessment

Take a moment to conduct a personal needs assessment. In your journal, list the situations that consistently challenge your boundaries. What are the common triggers? How do they make you feel? Next, brainstorm boundary adjustments you could implement to address these triggers. This exercise will help you tailor your boundaries to fit the unique dynamics of each situation, much like a tailor creating the perfect fit.

Adapting boundaries isn't just about protecting your time and energy; it's about creating spaces where you can thrive. When you take the time to tailor your boundaries, you're not just reacting to life's demands; you're shaping your life to reflect your values and needs. This isn't about building walls; it's about opening doors to a more balanced, fulfilling life.

Navigating Cultural Expectations and Boundaries

Growing up in a multicultural household was like living in a never-ending sitcom episode. My parents, hailing from different cultural backgrounds, often had their own unique takes on boundary-setting. Imagine the battle lines drawn over simple things like how to greet guests or who gets the last piece of cake. It was a constant juggling act of honoring traditions while trying to find my own voice. Cultural norms can profoundly shape how we perceive and establish boundaries, sometimes making it feel like you're balancing on a tightrope. In individualistic societies, personal autonomy is often celebrated, and boundaries are as clear as the labels on your favorite cereal box. However, collectivist cultures may emphasize community and family, leading to a more subtle and nuanced approach to boundary-setting.

Navigating family obligations is particularly challenging in collectivist cultures, where the family unit is often the sun around which everything else orbits. Imagine the scene for a second: your cousin calls, expecting you to attend her fifth cousin's wedding, and saying no feels akin to declaring you don't like puppies. Family obligations can blur the lines between personal choice and collective duty, making it challenging to assert individual preferences without feeling guilty. The pressure to conform to family expectations can leave you feeling boxed in as if your life choices are under perpetual review by a board of directors. In hierarchical societies, balancing respect and assertiveness can feel like a high-wire act where one misstep could lead to unintended consequences. Respecting authority is paramount, and any deviation from established norms is often met with disapproval. This can make boundary-setting an intricate dance, requiring a delicate blend of tact and clarity.

Establishing boundaries within these cultural frameworks demands a unique approach. Communication is key, and adapting your style to fit cultural norms can ensure understanding. For instance, in cultures where indirect communication is the norm, stating boundaries openly may be perceived as abrasive. Instead, use culturally appropriate cues or soft language to convey your needs. Sometimes, seeking allies within your cultural setting can provide invaluable support. These allies, who understand the cultural intricacies, can offer guidance and help you navigate the tricky waters of boundary-setting. They can also serve as intermediaries, helping to mediate conversations with family members or colleagues when necessary.

Let me share something fascinating about Samira, who grew up in a tight-knit community where family gatherings resembled a full-scale production, complete with a cast of hundreds. When she moved to a new city for work, she faced the challenge of balancing these family expectations with her burgeoning independence. Samira realized she needed to establish boundaries that respected her family's values while allowing her the space to grow. She started by communicating her needs with her family, explaining that while she cherished their traditions, she also needed time to focus on her career. Samira used her culturally appropriate communication skills, employing gentle language to express her desires without alienating her loved ones. She found allies in her cousins, who understood her predicament and supported her decisions. Over time, Samira discovered a balance that honored her cultural heritage while empowering her to pursue her goals.

Navigating cultural expectations is much like being a skilled navigator on a bustling sea, steering your ship while respecting the waves of tradition and the winds of change. By understanding the nuances of cultural norms and adapting your approach, you can set boundaries that honor both your heritage and your individuality. This chapter explores the delicate dance of cultural boundary-setting, offering insights and strategies for finding harmony in a world of diverse expectations. Whether you're balancing family obligations or asserting yourself in a hierarchical environment, the key lies in embracing your cultural identity while confidently expressing your needs.

Crafting Boundaries in Digital and Social Media Spaces

Digital boundaries. The mere phrase might conjure up images of an impenetrable wall around your social media accounts, keeping out those late-night cat meme marathons and unsolicited opinions from high school acquaintances. In today's hyper-connected world, maintaining personal boundaries becomes a formidable challenge when our lives are so intertwined with the digital realm. Gone are the days when the workday ended with the office lights dimming. Now, constant pings and notifications blur the lines between our personal and professional lives, turning what should be a sanctuary into a 24/7 helpline. The impact of this continuous connectivity on our mental well-being can be profound, leaving us feeling like a smartphone stuck in perpetual low-battery mode.

One of the most perplexing issues of digital boundary-setting is managing online privacy and personal information. It's like throwing a party and accidentally sending invitations to the entire neighborhood, only to have the one neighbor you were avoiding show up at the door. The internet doesn't forget; once your personal information is out there, it becomes a shared commodity. It's essential to be mindful of what you share, who you share it with, and the platforms you use. Whether it's that quirky photo from last year's holiday party or a heated comment on a discussion thread, every piece of content contributes to your digital footprint.

Then there's the notorious digital communication overload. We've all been there, that moment when your inbox resembles a circus tent with emails performing acrobatics every time you blink. Managing this deluge can feel like trying to stop a stampede with a feather duster. The sheer volume of digital messages - emails, texts, social media alerts - can leave you overwhelmed and anxious, constantly playing catch-up with your own life. It's a relentless cycle where your focus gets fragmented, and productivity takes a nosedive. The key is to recognize that just because technology enables constant communication doesn't mean you need to be on the receiving end 24/7.

So, how can you craft boundaries in this fast-paced digital landscape? For starters, consider setting digital detox periods to reclaim your time. Think of it as a mini-vacation for your brain, where you unplug from screens and plug into the world around you. Choose specific times during the day or week to disconnect from your devices, allowing yourself to recharge without the hum of notifications in the background. Some people find it helpful to declare a tech-free dinner hour or a quiet Sunday morning without screens. These moments of intentional disconnection can provide clarity and mental peace, reinforcing your boundaries.

Create personal guidelines for social media engagement. Social media is a double-edged sword, offering connection and information, but also comparison and pressure. It's easy to get sucked into the endless scroll, losing hours while your tea goes cold beside you. Establish rules for yourself, like limiting social media use to certain times of day or unfollowing accounts that leave you feeling inadequate. Remember, your online space is yours to curate and should reflect the values and boundaries you hold dear.

Take, for example, John, who found himself struggling with anxiety due to the constant barrage of social media notifications. He decided to implement a digital boundary plan, starting with setting specific times for checking his accounts and using apps to limit screen time. John also curated his online environment, unfollowing accounts that triggered stress and instead focusing on content that uplifted him. Over time, he noticed a significant improvement in his mental health and a newfound sense of control over his digital life.

The digital world offers endless possibilities, but navigating it requires a conscious effort to protect your mental and emotional well-being. Establishing boundaries in digital and social media spaces is not about cutting yourself off from technology but about using it in a way that enhances your life rather than detracts from it. As you craft your digital boundaries, remember that it's okay to step back, unplug, and take a breath. Your online presence should serve you, not the other way around.

Long-Term Boundary Maintenance Strategies

Imagine setting boundaries as planting a garden. The initial effort is rewarding, but your flourishing plot can quickly turn into a tangled mess of weeds without regular care. Much like a garden, boundary-setting is not a one-time affair. It requires consistent attention and adjustments to keep it thriving. As we continue to grow and change, so too should our boundaries. What worked for you a year ago might not be cutting it today. Consistency is your best ally in ensuring these boundaries remain steadfast over time. It's about setting clear expectations and sticking to them, even when life throws its inevitable curveballs. Think of it as your personal constitution—a set of rules that govern how you interact with the world, providing a sense of stability amidst chaos.

However, maintaining boundaries long-term is not without its challenges. Complacency is one of the biggest culprits, often sneaking in like an uninvited guest at a party. Over time, the initial vigor with which we set our boundaries can fade, leading to a gradual erosion of our intentions. It's easy to slip back into old habits when life gets busy, and before you know it, your boundaries start looking like Swiss cheese—full of holes. Not to mention the external pressures that constantly push us to relax our boundaries. Whether it's a demanding boss who doesn't understand the concept of work-life balance or well-meaning family members who equate love with constant availability, these pressures can make it difficult to uphold the boundaries we've worked so hard to establish.

To keep your boundaries effective and resilient, regular reviews and adjustments are key. Much like a car needs regular servicing to run smoothly, your boundaries require periodic check-ins to ensure they're still serving you well. Take time to reflect on the boundaries you've set. Are they still aligned with your values and needs? Have any new situations arisen that require a shift in your approach? Adjusting your boundaries based on these reflections ensures they remain relevant and functional. Establishing accountability systems can also be incredibly beneficial. Whether it's enlisting a friend to check in on your progress or using a journal to track your boundary-setting successes and challenges, accountability provides the support and motivation needed to stick to your guns.

Here's what unfolded when Becky, a young professional who, after a particularly overwhelming year, made the decision to set boundaries around her work hours. Initially, Becky was diligent about leaving her office by six each evening, ensuring she had time for herself and her family. However, as months passed and her workload increased, she found herself slipping back into old habits, staying late at the office more often than not. Realizing the need for change, Becky started scheduling monthly reflections to reassess her boundaries. She also partnered with a colleague to hold each other accountable, celebrating successes and addressing slip-ups together. This newfound commitment to her boundaries not only improved Becky's work-life balance but also enhanced her overall well-being.

Ultimately, long-term boundary maintenance is about creating a sustainable system that supports your life's dynamic nature. It's about being adaptable while staying true to your core values. By regularly evaluating and adjusting your boundaries, you create a framework that evolves with you, ensuring you remain in control of your time, energy, and resources. This sets the stage for a life where boundaries are not a burden but a means of empowerment, allowing you to navigate your world with confidence and clarity.

As you embrace these strategies, remember that boundaries are not just about saying no; they're about saying yes to a life that reflects your true self. In the next chapter, we'll explore how to integrate these boundary-setting skills into everyday life, ensuring they become second nature and seamlessly enhance your relationships, work, and personal pursuits.

SUSTAINING CHANGE AND PERSONAL GROWTH

PICTURE YOUR LIFE AS a garden. Some days, you're the proud gardener, basking in the sun, marveling at the blooms of your labor. Other days, you're knee-deep in weeds, wondering why you ever thought you could keep a plant alive. Personal growth is a lot like that garden—it requires constant care, attention, and, yes, sometimes a little bit of weeding. This chapter is all about nurturing that garden, embracing continuous personal growth, and learning how to sustain the changes you've worked so hard to make.

Embracing lifelong learning is the fertilizer for this garden. It's the act of continually seeking knowledge and skills, not just for career advancement but for personal fulfillment, too. Lifelong learning is about being curious, like when you were a kid and wondered why the sky was blue or why your goldfish seemed to stare at you. By keeping that curiosity alive, you enhance your adaptability, confidence, and overall quality of life. Whether it's picking up a new hobby, learning a new language, or simply reading a book that broadens your perspective, these activities contribute to your personal growth.

Now, setting personal development goals is like mapping out which plants you want in your garden. It gives direction and purpose, ensuring you're not just watering weeds. Break these goals into manageable chunks, like deciding to learn a new skill every month. Engage in regular skill-building activities, whether it's taking an online course or attending a weekend workshop. These activities are like the sunshine and rain your garden needs to thrive. Online courses and workshops offer a buffet of knowledge at your fingertips, while books and podcasts serve as the seasoned gardeners sharing their wisdom.

Cultivating a growth mindset is crucial. It's about viewing challenges as opportunities rather than as roadblocks. Reflective exercises can help foster this mindset, allowing you to see setbacks as stepping stones. Think of it like composting—transforming what might initially seem like waste into something that enriches your garden. So grab your metaphorical trowel, dig deep, and embrace the messy, rewarding process of continuous personal development.

Interactive Element: Personal Development Plan

Take a moment to jot down three new skills or hobbies you'd like to explore. Next, outline a plan for how you'll incorporate these into your schedule. Consider resources like online courses or local workshops. Reflect on how each new skill can contribute to your personal growth, much like the way different plants add beauty and diversity to a garden.

Reflecting on Boundary Progress and Adjustments

Imagine you're watching reruns of your life's sitcom, and you're the star. Each episode is a chance to reflect on your boundary-setting antics. Reflecting on how you've managed your boundaries isn't just about replaying your greatest hits (or misses). It's a way to see where you've succeeded and where you might need a plot twist. Regular reflection is like a personal director's commentary, helping you identify what worked, what didn't, and how you can improve. It's a vital part of maintaining and refining your boundaries, allowing you to spot patterns and adjust your script for future episodes. Self-assessment is more than just a buzzword—it's your ticket to personal growth, helping you stay aligned with your authentic self.

One of the best tools for this reflection process is a boundary-setting journal. This isn't your teenage diary filled with musings about your crushes and existential dread. Instead, it's a place to document your boundary experiences, victories, and lessons. Each entry is a snapshot of your boundary progress, a mirror reflecting your growth and areas that need attention. Regular self-check-ins, much like those annoying but necessary oil changes, keep your boundary engine running smoothly. They help you stay in tune with your needs and ensure your boundaries remain relevant and effective. By taking a moment to jot down your thoughts and feelings, you create a roadmap for navigating your boundary landscape.

Flexibility is key in boundary-setting. Life has a way of throwing curveballs, and your boundaries need to adapt to those changes. Just like adjusting your sails on a windy day, recognizing when your boundaries need reevaluation is crucial. Strategies for modifying boundaries involve listening to feedback from yourself and others. For instance, if you notice that a boundary is causing more stress than peace, it might be time to tweak it. Let's rewind and take a look at Anna, who realized her rigid work boundaries were stifling her creativity. By adjusting them, she found a balance that allowed her to thrive both professionally and personally. Anna's story is a testament to the power of reflection and adjustment.

Building a Community of Boundary-Setters

This might remind you of something familiar: you're at a party, and the DJ is playing your favorite song. But instead of dancing, you're stuck on the sidelines, feeling like everyone else is in on a secret you've missed. That's what boundary-setting can feel like when you're going at it alone. But here's the thing: you don't have to tackle it solo. Building a community of boundary-setters is like finding your dance crew—people who get you, who encourage you to take the floor, and who cheer you on when you're nailing those tricky moves. Connecting with others who share similar goals can provide the encouragement and accountability you need to keep practicing your boundary-setting skills, even when the music gets complicated.

Shared experiences within a community are a powerful thing. They remind you that you're not the only one who sometimes struggles with saying no or feels like a pushover. These shared stories of triumph and tribulation empower you and help you see that setbacks aren't the end of the world. They're just part of the process. So how do you find this magical community? Start by joining support groups or online forums where boundary-setting is a common theme. These spaces are filled with people eager to share their insights and learn from each other. Attending workshops or networking events focused on self-development can also be a great way to meet like-minded individuals, much like finding fellow bookworms at a library event.

Being part of a supportive community doesn't just bolster your boundary-setting skills; it opens doors to collective growth. Engaging in group discussions and activities exposes you to diverse perspectives and insights you might not encounter on your own. It's like having a potluck dinner where everyone brings a unique dish to the table, broadening your understanding and expanding your toolkit with new strategies and ideas. Take the story of Jake, who joined a local boundary-setting group. Through shared stories and mutual support, he not only improved his own boundary skills but also helped others, creating a ripple effect of empowerment.

Reinforcing New Habits and Behaviors

Picture the process of setting boundaries as a dance. At first, your steps may be hesitant and awkward, but with practice, they become second nature. This is where habit reinforcement comes into play. Just like learning a new dance routine, reinforcing consistent practices is crucial for making boundary-setting an automatic part of your daily life. Repetition is the unsung hero in this process, transforming each step from clumsy to graceful with time and persistence. By regularly rehearsing your boundary-setting moves, you train your mind and body to respond instinctively, even when the spotlight is on you.

To solidify these new habits, consider using habit trackers as your personal dance coach. These handy tools, whether digital or on paper, help you monitor daily progress and keep your motivation high. They provide a visual reminder of your commitment, nudging you to stay on track. Setting reminders and cues around your environment also reinforces these practices, like placing sticky notes on your fridge or phone to remind you of your personal promises. These gentle nudges act as a steadfast partner, ensuring you don't miss a beat, even when life throws unexpected challenges your way.

Challenges? Oh, they'll show up, all right, like an uninvited guest at a party. Common triggers that disrupt your carefully crafted habits might include stress, unexpected changes, or those delightful moments when you're simply too tired to care. The trick is to identify these potential saboteurs early on. Recognizing them allows you to devise strategies to handle disruptions, like having a backup plan for those days when your routine goes sideways. Over time, these strategies help you navigate the inevitable hiccups, keeping your boundary dance in rhythm.

Let me paint the picture of Laura, a mother and freelance writer who struggled to maintain a work-life balance. She used habit trackers to carve out time for writing, family, and self-care. By setting clear daily goals and reminders, Laura gradually turned her chaotic schedule into a well-choreographed routine. Her story illustrates how committed practice and strategic adjustments can transform your boundary-setting from a struggle into a seamless dance, where every step is guided by intention and resilience.

Celebrating Successes and Learning from Setbacks

Imagine boundary-setting as a game of chess, where each move requires strategy and foresight. Every time you successfully set a boundary, it's like capturing a knight or a bishop—a small victory in the grand game of life. Recognizing these successes is crucial. It's tempting to brush aside our wins, considering them insignificant, but each one is a building block for confidence and future success. Celebrating these achievements motivates us to persist, reinforcing our commitment to maintaining boundaries. Positive reinforcement, like a pat on the back, encourages continued effort and turns boundary-setting from a chore into a rewarding experience.

So, how do we celebrate these victories without sounding like we're throwing a parade every time we say "no" to an unnecessary coffee date? Simple strategies can make a world of difference. Try creating a success journal. Jot down every instance where you've stood your ground. Over time, this journal becomes a visual testament to your progress. Reward yourself for reaching milestones, whether it's a quiet evening with a favorite book or a weekend getaway. These small acts of celebration serve as reminders that you're worth the effort and that each boundary crossed is a step toward your best self.

Of course, life isn't just about victories. Setbacks happen, and they can feel as deflating as a flat tire on a road trip. But here's the twist: setbacks are incredibly valuable. They offer insights that triumphs never could. Each stumble is a lesson wrapped in a slightly bruised ego. Reflecting on these setbacks helps identify areas for improvement, much like a post-game analysis. Let me walk you through what happened with Mike, who initially struggled with setting boundaries at work. Instead of letting setbacks defeat him, he analyzed where things went awry. This reflection turned his missteps into stepping stones, guiding him to refine his approach and ultimately succeed. Mike's experience illustrates how setbacks can be catalysts for profound growth, teaching us resilience and adaptability in the face of adversity.

Maintaining Momentum in Boundary-Setting

When you first start setting boundaries, it can feel like a breath of fresh air—a personal revolution. But keeping that momentum going? That's where the real work begins. It's like deciding to run a marathon after finally managing to jog around the block without wheezing. Sustaining momentum in boundary-setting is crucial because it turns temporary change into a lasting lifestyle. It requires ongoing motivation and consistent effort, much like watering a plant regularly to prevent it from wilting. Consistency is the secret sauce in achieving long-term goals. It takes those initial sparks of inspiration and turns them into a steady flame capable of withstanding the winds of life.

Setting short-term goals can help keep your focus sharp to maintain this momentum. Think of these as the stepping stones across a river. They guide you, keeping your eyes on the next step rather than the entire journey. Regular self-reflection and goal reviews serve as checkpoints, helping you adjust your path as needed. Imagine them as pit stops in a long race where you can refuel and reassess your strategy. These moments of introspection ensure you're not just moving for the sake of movement but progressing in a direction that aligns with your core values and desires.

Of course, life isn't always smooth sailing. There are bound to be obstacles that threaten to derail your progress. Recognizing signs of burnout is particularly important. It can sneak up on you like a cat ready to pounce, leaving you drained and demotivated. Taking preventive action is essential, whether it means scheduling regular downtime or seeking support when needed. The key is to listen to your body and mind, addressing fatigue before it morphs into something more serious.

Dig deeper into the tale of Rachel, who started setting boundaries in her work life to prevent burnout. She began with simple goals, such as not replying to work emails after hours. Over time, she built on these successes, reinforcing her resolve through regular self-assessment. Rachel's commitment to maintaining momentum ensured that her new habits became second nature, helping her achieve a healthier work-life balance. Her journey illustrates that with dedication and the right strategies, sustaining momentum in boundary-setting is not only possible but immensely rewarding, transforming fleeting wins into lasting triumphs.

Preparing for Future Challenges with Confidence

Here's how this might play out in everyday life: you're on a road trip, cruising along the scenic route, when suddenly the GPS throws a tantrum, and you find yourself lost on a winding road. Boundary setting can feel a bit like that sometimes—smooth sailing until life tosses a curveball your way. But here's the thing: challenges in boundary-setting are as inevitable as detours on a road trip. Anticipating these potential obstacles is like packing a spare tire and snacks; it enhances your resilience and keeps you confident when things get bumpy. By planning for these challenges, you lay the groundwork for bouncing back with grace and grit.

Developing a proactive mindset means arming yourself with strategies before the storm hits. Think of it as creating a contingency plan for your boundaries. Consider potential scenarios where your limits might be tested—perhaps a colleague who constantly interrupts your lunch hour or a family member who drops by unannounced. Once you've identified these scenarios, craft a plan to maintain your boundaries. Maybe it involves practicing assertive communication or setting clear expectations in advance. Having a plan is like carrying an umbrella on a cloudy day—you might not need it, but you'll be glad to have it if the skies open up.

Confidence is the secret sauce that helps you overcome challenges and maintain your boundaries. Building confidence is much like strengthening a muscle; it requires regular exercise and practice. Confidence-building exercises and affirmations can play a pivotal role in reinforcing your belief in your ability to set and uphold boundaries. Imagine standing in front of a mirror, affirming, "I deserve respect, and my boundaries matter." It might feel silly at first, but over time, these affirmations become the foundation of your self-assurance. When challenges arise, this confidence propels you forward, reminding you that you have the tools and resilience needed to navigate any boundary obstacle.

Take the story of Lucy, who faced constant demands from her boss that threatened her work-life balance. By anticipating these challenges and developing a plan to communicate her limits, Lucy successfully maintained her boundaries without sacrificing her career. Her confidence grew as she realized her ability to handle challenges with poise. Lucy's experience shows that with preparation and confidence, you can easily navigate future challenges, ensuring your boundaries remain intact.

Living Authentically Through Empowered Boundaries

Living authentically is like finally wearing an outfit that fits perfectly—comfortable, flattering, and entirely your style. It's about aligning your boundaries with your true values and goals, creating a life that feels like it truly belongs to you. These boundaries are not just lines in the sand; they are reflections of your identity, guiding you to live in harmony with who you genuinely are. Imagine boundaries as the frame of a masterpiece, highlighting the vibrant colors of your beliefs and dreams. By setting boundaries that resonate with your core values, you ensure that every decision, big or small, honors your personal integrity.

Embracing authenticity means expressing yourself without fear of judgment. It's about speaking your truth, even if your voice shakes slightly. It's about making choices that reflect your genuine self, not the self that others expect or demand. This might mean politely declining a weekend event to recharge, or stepping up to defend your perspective in a meeting, knowing that your voice matters. Practicing self-expression involves trusting that who you are is enough and that your boundaries are valid. This leap into authenticity can feel daunting, but it's incredibly liberating. It's like opening a window to let the fresh air in, clearing out the stale expectations and pressures that cloud your true self.

The beauty of living authentically is the fulfillment and satisfaction it brings. As you align your boundaries with your authentic self, you experience a profound increase in self-awareness and confidence. You begin to understand what truly matters to you, and this clarity guides your path. Consider the story of Mia, who once felt trapped by the expectations of others. By setting empowered boundaries, she gradually peeled back the layers of external demands and discovered her passion for art. Her journey of self-discovery led to a transformation, where Mia not only pursued her creative dreams but also built relationships grounded in mutual respect and understanding.

Living authentically through empowered boundaries is a continuous process of self-discovery and growth. It's about embracing the unique person you are and allowing that authenticity to shape your life. By setting boundaries that honor your true self, you create a foundation for a fulfilling and meaningful existence where your values lead the way. As you continue on this path, remember that each step taken in authenticity is a step toward a life that reflects the real you. Now, with these insights, you are ready to move forward with clarity and strength as you navigate the way forward.

Conclusion

Well, here we are at the end of our journey together. I hope you've found this book on boundary-setting both enlightening and a little bit entertaining. If you're feeling a mix of relief and empowerment, you're in good company. Boundaries are like the invisible superheroes of our lives, quietly working behind the scenes to enhance our personal autonomy and improve our mental and emotional well-being. They're not just barriers but bridges to healthier relationships and a more balanced life.

Throughout this book, we've explored a wide array of topics, each one a stepping stone on your path to empowered boundary-setting. We began by diving into the nature of boundaries, understanding how they function and why they are essential. We've tackled their psychological roots and cultural influences, giving you a well-rounded perspective on how boundaries are perceived across different contexts.

We've delved into emotional resilience and self-care, emphasizing how these concepts serve as the backbone for effective boundary-setting. Communication, as you've learned, is the key to expressing and maintaining boundaries without feeling like a dictator or a doormat. Remember the techniques we discussed, like assertive communication and the art of saying no with grace. These are your tools for navigating tricky conversations and maintaining your boundaries with confidence.

Overcoming fear and guilt has been another crucial part of our exploration. It's easy to feel weighed down by others' expectations, but I hope you now see these feelings as opportunities for growth rather than obstacles. Integrating boundaries into your daily life is not just about saying no; it's about saying yes to the things that truly matter to you.

As you reflect on your progress, take a moment to acknowledge the personal growth and transformation you've experienced. You may have started this journey feeling unsure or overwhelmed. But look at you now—armed with the knowledge and skills to set boundaries that honor your true self. This transformation is a testament to your dedication and willingness to embrace change.

Boundary setting is not a one-and-done deal. It's an ongoing practice, much like tending to a garden. Some days, you'll find weeds; other days, you'll marvel at the blooms. My call to action is simple: keep at it. Consistency and adaptability are your allies in this journey. As life changes, so too will your boundaries. Embrace this fluidity and continue refining your skills.

Remember, you're not alone. Seek out communities of like-minded individuals who are also on this path. Shared experiences can be incredibly powerful, providing motivation and accountability when the going gets tough. Whether it's a local support group or an online forum, connecting with others can be a source of strength and encouragement.

I want to leave you with an empowering thought: you have the ability to live authentically through empowered boundaries. The changes you've made are just the beginning. Look forward to a future filled with personal growth and fulfillment. You have the tools, the knowledge, and the courage to create a life that reflects your values and desires.

Lastly, thank you for allowing me to guide you on this journey. Your commitment to personal development inspires me, and I am grateful for the opportunity to support you. Remember, this book is a starting point. Continue exploring the vast world of boundary-setting and personal growth. There are countless resources and communities out there ready to support you.

As we part ways, know that I'm cheering you on. May your boundaries be firm, your heart be open, and your path be fulfilling. Here's to living life on your terms!

REFERENCES

BetterHelp. (n.d.). *The importance of setting boundaries: 10 benefits for you and your relationships.* Retrieved from https://www.betterhelp.com/advice/general/the-importance-of-setting -boundaries-10-benefits-for-you-and-your-relationships/

EndCAN. (2023, October 23). *The importance of setting boundaries as an adult survivor of child abuse.* Retrieved from https://endcan.org/2023/10/23/the-importance-of-setting-boundaries-as-an -adult-survivor-of-child-abuse/#:~:text=Without%20exposure%20to%20healt hy%20boundaries,overcoming%20the%20effects%20of%20abuse.

HollyPhD. (n.d.). *The art of boundaries: A cultural perspective on setting boundaries.* Retrieved from https://www.hollyphd.com/blog/the-art-of-boundaries-a-cultural-perspective -on-setting-boundaries#:~:text=Interpersonal%20Challenges%3A%20Misund erstandings%20can%20occur,aggressive%2C%20potentially%20leading%20to %20conflict.

Pennycooke, M. (n.d.). *7 myths about setting boundaries.* Retrieved from https://makedapennycooke.com/7-myths-setting-boundaries/#:~:text=Your% 20boundaries%20are%20not%20a,same%20as%20causing%20them%20harm.

Mayo Clinic. (n.d.). *Resilience: Build skills to endure hardship.* Retrieved from

https://www.mayoclinic.org/tests-procedures/resilience-training/in-depth/res
ilience/art-20046311#:~:text=Resilience%20can%20help%20protect%20you,b
eing%20bullied%20or%20having%20trauma.

National Institute of Mental Health. (n.d.). *Caring for your mental health.* Retrieved from https://www.nimh.nih.gov/health/topics/caring-for-your-m
ental-health

Mayo Clinic. (n.d.). *Mindfulness exercises.* Retrieved from https://www.mayoclinic.org/healthy-lifestyle/consumer-health/in-dept
h/mindfulness-exercises/art-20046356

Emotional Badass. (n.d.). *The truth about boundaries, peace, and maturity: Improving mental health in highly sensitive people.* Retrieved from https://www.emotionalbadass.com/podcast/the-truth-about-boundaries-peac
e-and-maturity-improving-mental-health-in-highly-sensitive-people#:~:text=T
he%20Role%20of%20Boundaries%20in,%2Dcare%20and%20self%2Dimprov
ement.

Verywell Mind. (n.d.). *Assertive communication: What it means and how to use it.* Retrieved from https://www.verywellmind.com/learn-assertive-comm
unication-in-five-simple-steps-3144969

Simply Psychology. (n.d.). *Emotional labor: Examples & consequences.* Retrieved from https://www.simplypsychology.org/emotional-labor.html

Psychology Today. (2023, September). *4 ways to deal with energy vampires.* Retrieved from https://www.psychologytoday.com/us/blog/click-here-for-ha
ppiness/202309/strategies-to-deal-with-energy-vampires

Centerstone. (n.d.). *Balancing empathy and self-care.* Retrieved from https://centerstone.org/our-resources/health-wellness/balancing-empat
hy-and-self-care/

Simply Midori. (n.d.). *The psychology behind people-pleasing: Why we fear disapproval.* Retrieved from https://simplymidori.com/why-we-fear-disappro
val/

PubMed Central. (n.d.). *Shame and guilt-proneness as mediators.* Retrieved from https://pmc.ncbi.nlm.nih.gov/articles/PMC5362253/

Dave Bailey. (n.d.). *How to deliver constructive feedback in difficult situations.* Retrieved from https://www.dave-bailey.com/blog/nonviolent-communication

BetterUp. (n.d.). *How self-compassion strengthens resilience.* Retrieved from https://www.betterup.com/blog/how-self-compassion-strengthens-resilience

Marriage & Family Services. (n.d.). *Cultivating healthy boundaries in family dynamics.* Retrieved from https://www.marriagefamilyservices.com/post/cultivating-healthy-boundaries-in-family-dynamics/#:~:text=The%20Role%20of%20Healthy%20Boundaries,and%20promoting%20emotional%20well%2Dbeing

HelpGuide. (n.d.). *Setting healthy boundaries in relationships.* Retrieved from https://www.helpguide.org/relationships/social-connection/setting-healthy-boundaries-in-relationships

The Muse. (n.d.). *How to say no to anyone (even a good friend).* Retrieved from https://www.themuse.com/advice/how-to-say-no-to-anyone-even-a-good-friend

Banner Health. (n.d.). *How to survive the stress of family gatherings.* Retrieved from https://www.bannerhealth.com/healthcareblog/advise-me/agree-to-disagree-and-other-tips-for-surviving-family-gatherings

Asana. (2024). *12 tips for effective communication in the workplace.* Retrieved from https://asana.com/resources/effective-communication-workplace

Forbes Business Council. (2024, September 17). *Workplace stress: Causes, impacts, and solutions.* Retrieved from https://www.forbes.com/councils/forbesbusinesscouncil/2024/09/17/workplace-stress-causes-impacts-and-solutions/

Remote.com. (n.d.). *Mastering work-life balance when you work from home.* Retrieved from https://remote.com/blog/remote-work-life-balance

Verywell Mind. (n.d.). *Empathic overload: How to ground and regulate in a world of intense emotions.* Retrieved from https://heididellaire.com/empathic-overload-how-to-ground-and-regulate-in-a-world-of-intense-emotions/

Verywell Mind. (n.d.). *8 ways to stop being a people-pleaser.* Retrieved from https://www.verywellmind.com/how-to-stop-being-a-people-pleaser-5184412

Mindful Health Solutions. (n.d.). *How to break free from and avoid toxic relationships for better mental health.* Retrieved from https://mindfulhealthsolutions.com/how-to-break-free-from-and-avoid-toxic-relationships-for-better-mental-health/

Becoming Who You Are. (n.d.). *How to cultivate boundaries for a truly authentic life.* Retrieved from https://www.becomingwhoyouare.net/how-to-cultivate-boundaries-for-a-truly-authentic-life/

PubMed Central. (n.d.). *The sense of self in the aftermath of trauma: Lessons learned.* Retrieved from https://pmc.ncbi.nlm.nih.gov/articles/PMC7594748/

Talkspace. (n.d.). *How to stop being codependent: 10 tips to overcome it.* Retrieved from https://www.talkspace.com/blog/how-to-stop-being-codependent/

Relias. (n.d.). *Autonomy, connection, and healing vicarious trauma in direct support.* Retrieved from https://www.relias.com/blog/autonomy-connection-healing-vicarious-trauma-direct-support

Manoshala. (n.d.). *The importance of setting boundaries for emotional health.* Retrieved from https://www.manoshala.com/post/the-importance-of-setting-boundaries-for-emotional-health

Penn Foundation. (n.d.). *10 daily habits for mental wellness.* Retrieved from https://www.pennfoundation.org/news-events/articles-of-interest/10-daily-habits-for-mental-wellness/

Miriam Learning Center. (n.d.). *Strategies for establishing healthy technology boundaries.* Retrieved from https://www.miriamstl.org/aboutmiriam/news/post-details/board/blogs/post/strategies-for-establishing-healthy-technology-boundaries#::text=Set%20Digital%20Boundaries%26text=Utilize%20built%2Din%20tools%20like,usage%20and%20manage%20screen%20time

Ezra. (n.d.). *The importance of self-care routines.* Retrieved from https://ezra.com/blog/the-importance-of-self-care-routines

Positive Psychology. (n.d.). *How to set healthy boundaries: Build great self-care habits*. Retrieved from https://positivepsychology.com/great-self-care-setting-healthy-boundaries/

Holly PhD. (n.d.). *The art of boundaries: A cultural perspective*. Retrieved from https://www.hollyphd.com/blog/the-art-of-boundaries-a-cultural-perspective-on-setting-boundaries#:~:text=For%20instance%2C%20many%20Western%20cultures,more%20subtle%20boundary%2Dsetting%20practices

Lifeat.io. (n.d.). *Building digital boundaries: A step-by-step guide to reclaiming your time and focus*. Retrieved from https://lifeat.io/blog/building-digital-boundaries-a-step-by-step-guide-to-reclaiming-your-time-and-focus

Fair Play Talks. (2023, January 13). *Setting boundaries vital for work-life balance, study shows*. Retrieved from https://www.fairplaytalks.com/2023/01/13/setting-professional-work-boundaries-vital-for-work-life-balance-say-quiet-quitters/

Counseling Today. (n.d.). *The sensitivity of boundary setting in collectivist cultures*. Retrieved from https://www.counseling.org/publications/counseling-today-magazine/article-archive/article/legacy/the-sensitivity-of-boundary-setting-in-collectivist-cultures

Johnson & Wales University Online. (n.d.). *Lifelong learning: What it is and why it matters*. Retrieved from https://online.jwu.edu/blog/lifelong-learning-what-it-is-and-why-it-matters/

Therapy with Olivia. (n.d.). *On boundaries: A therapist's guide on setting healthy boundaries*. Retrieved from https://www.therapywitholivia.com/blog/a-therapists-guide-on-setting-healthy-boundaries

PubMed Central. (n.d.). *Community boundary spanners as an addition to the health workforce*. Retrieved from https://www.ncbi.nlm.nih.gov/pmc/articles/PMC6131945/

Verywell Mind. (n.d.). *Behavior modification: Techniques for positive change*. Retrieved from https://www.verywellmind.com/behavior-modification-techniques-8622711

THE ART OF SETTING BOUNDARIES

You've taken the first steps toward saying "no" with confidence, managing stress, and focusing on what truly matters. Now, you have everything you need to create the balance and peace you deserve in your life.

But your journey doesn't stop here.

By sharing your honest opinion of this book, you can help others—just like you—who are searching for ways to set boundaries and regain control of their lives.

Why leave a review?

Your words matter. By sharing your thoughts, you'll:

- Show others where they can find the same guidance and support.

- Inspire someone else to take their first step toward setting boundaries.

- Keep the conversation about boundaries alive, making it easier for others to feel empowered in their journey.

Here's how you can help:

Simply click the link below or scan the attached QR code to leave your review on Amazon:

Click here to leave your review on Amazon.

Thank you for helping to create a world where setting boundaries isn't a challenge—it's a way of life. Your review will guide others to the support they need and help keep this important topic alive.

With gratitude,

Alex Harper